Midwestern Miscellany

LIII
Issue 1
SPRING
2025

I0558034

Lisel Mueller

Guest Editor
Linda Nemec Foster

The Midwestern Press

Copy Editing and Design
Patricia Oman

Midwestern Miscellany (ISSN 0885-4742) is a peer-reviewed journal published twice a year (Spring and Fall) by the Society for the Study of Midwestern Literature.

The journal is a member of the Council of Editors of Learned Journals.

In honor of
Lisel Mueller

CONTENTS

PREFACE

Linda Nemec Foster

This issue of *Midwestern Miscellany* is dedicated to Lisel Mueller (1924–2020), whose brilliant poetry spanned nearly four decades, was published in nine volumes (as well as two books of translation), and garnered nearly every major literary prize in America—including the Lamont Poetry Prize (1975), the National Book Award (1980), the Carl Sandburg Award (1990), a National Endowment for the Arts fellowship (1990), the Ruth Lilly Poetry Prize (2002), and the Pulitzer Prize for her master work *Alive Together: New and Selected Poems* (1996). When anyone asks me, in my opinion, what is the best book of poetry—or, more accurately, the most essential book of poetry—that has been published in America within the last thirty years, I answer without hesitation: *Alive Together* by Lisel Mueller.

And, when various strangers at literary events ask me: "Are you Linda Nemec Foster, the person that Lisel Mueller dedicated the poem, 'Why We Tell Stories,' to?" I proudly (and humbly) say "yes." Proudly, because this poem that has been widely anthologized and praised for many years is such a superb achievement of nuanced metaphor, pacing, and resonance. Humbly, because Mueller always said I inspired the poem. She drafted "Why We Tell Stories" in the fall of 1977 when I was her student in graduate school; she sent me a copy of her final revision dated October 5, 1977. I still have that revision tucked into my copy of *Alive Together*. (The poem was first published in *Poetry* and was included in her Pulitzer Prize–winning volume.)

I met Lisel Mueller in July 1977 when I selected her—and, more importantly, she selected me—to work with as my faculty advisor in the ground-breaking MFA Program for Creative Writers at Goddard College in Vermont.[1] I describe it as ground-breaking because it was the first low-residency MFA program in the country, established by Ellen Bryant Voigt in the mid-1970s. During my tenure in the program from 1977 to 1979, Voigt had gathered an extraordinary group of poets and writers as faculty members: Raymond Carver, Louise Glück, John Irving, Donald Hall, Heather McHugh, Stephen Dobyns, Tobias Wolff, Rosellen Brown, Robert Hass, Barbara Greenberg … and Lisel Mueller.

I was immediately drawn to Mueller's work. Her poetry, often in short, lyrical form, is imbued with a sense of history: she was born in Hamburg, Germany, and emigrated with her family to America in the summer of 1939, just before Hitler invaded Poland and ignited the catastrophe of World War II. The family settled in the Midwest—first in Evansville, Indiana, and later in the Chicago area—but the history of her native country had a profound effect on her poetry and her view of the world. As poet Reginald Gibbons said, "She was not a tragic poet at all. But underneath it … there was that basement of memories and knowledge of cataclysm" (17).

However, it's important to know that the subjects in her accessible yet intricately layered poems reflect a wide range: of landscape and place, time and family, art and music, language and perception, fairy tales and myth. Mueller studied folk and fairy tales as a graduate student at Indiana University, and I was intrigued by this aspect of her education that was reflected in so much of her work.

During my first semester as her student, I concentrated on writing a sequence of poems inspired by the Russian witch Baba Yaga. Mueller was the perfect faculty advisor as she used her vast knowledge of fairy tales to guide my creative writing and critical reading. She recommended a superb list of books for me to read: not only rare collections of fairy tales from around the world, but also critical analyses of the cultural, societal, and psychological underpinnings of the genre. One of the books on my reading list included a folk tale titled "Why We Tell Stories." When I wrote my annotated bibliography on the book and sent it to Mueller for evaluation, she said she was inspired by the title of the tale to write a response. So, using the same title, "Why We Tell Stories," for her new poem, Mueller created a brilliant and haunting answer. "Because we used to have leaves" is the first line. "[B]ecause our children believe / they can fly" is another (lines 6–7). "[B]ecause we had survived / sisters and brothers, daughters and sons, / we discovered bones that rose / ... as white birds in the trees" (lines 26–30). The entire poem is about time and movement, the past and the present, and the arc of narrative that connects us to the future. It's a stunning poem, and I was so moved when Mueller dedicated it to me.

After I graduated from the MFA program at Goddard in 1979, my relationship with Lisel Mueller evolved from that of a mentor to a confidante to a cherished friend. Our relationship deepened over the years as my husband, children, and I would visit her and her husband Paul frequently every year. As a matter of fact, my daughter Ellen and I were visiting Mueller in early April 1997 when she got the wonderful news that she won the Pulitzer Prize in Poetry for *Alive Together*. What an amazing celebration that was!

Mueller and I remained close the remainder of her life. My husband Tony and I visited her in late January 2020 in her nursing home facility in Chicago on West Foster Avenue (a wonderful coincidence that we would often joke about). Several weeks later, she passed. I remember getting the call from her daughter Jenny with the sad news. Yes, Mueller's health was failing, but when we saw her that last time, her face was radiant, her embrace was welcoming. She kept kissing my hand and asking me when I would return. At the time, I didn't know it would be my last visit.

Her passing has left an absence in my life. Of course, I have her poems and the lovely gifts she has given me over the years: jewelry, books, small artifacts. And the wonderful memories: attending plays at the Steppenwolf Theatre; visiting the Field Museum and Shedd Aquarium with our son and daughter in tow; a boat ride on Lake Geneva, Wisconsin; a Renaissance Festival; dinners at The Berghoff Restaurant on W. Adams Street and Francesca's on Bryn Mawr. And the countless visits to the grand Art Institute of Chicago on Michigan Avenue. But, to quote that simple line from Morgan Freeman in *The Shawshank Redemption*, "I just miss my friend."

When Marcia Noe approached me to be the Guest Editor for this special issue of the *Midwestern Miscellany*, I could not refuse. Even though I do not consider myself an academic. Even though I have never guest-edited a scholarly journal before. I wanted to honor Lisel Mueller's poetry and legacy. Both Noe and I agree that her work is not that well known—even in the current poetry world, let alone the general public. We are hoping this issue reignites a deeper and widespread interest and appreciation for this extraordinary poet, who, as one scholar told me, is a hidden gem under the radar of contemporary poetry.

In this issue, you will find Janet Ruth Heller's analysis of Mueller's midwestern subjects and themes. Elizabeth Iannaci discusses her very personal perspective on one of Mueller's most iconic poems, "Monet Refuses the Operation." Anita Skeen reflects on Mueller's influence on her career as a teacher and poet. Elaine Terranova offers an appreciation of Mueller's lyric and narrative impulses in her poems. The final essay, written by Mueller's daughter Jenny, discusses in depth—for the first time—a very fascinating and little-known chapter of her mother's life. The essays are followed by a generous selection of twenty of the most evocative poems from Mueller's Pulitzer Prize–winning book *Alive Together*.

In 2021, the year after Mueller died, New Issues Press published my twelfth collection of poems, *The Blue Divide*. (The second edition was published by Cornerstone Press in 2024.) I dedicated the book to her. In an interview discussing the collection, a reviewer noted that the dedication line reads "for Lisel Mueller" not "in memoriam for Lisel Mueller." He asked me why, and I responded, "She is still alive for me. I dearly miss her physical presence, but I do not consider her gone. Lisel is very much with me—a constant inspiration—as she was for almost 43 years."

When I think about Mueller's profound influence on my poetry, my teaching, my life (and even the lives of my family: my husband and children), I cannot help but reflect on the poem she dedicated to me, "Why We Tell Stories." How her dear spirit lives on in those words. How I remember her generous heart resonating in the poem's last lines. The lines that bridge the present and the future with the poem's last emphatic word:

and though we listen only

haphazardly, with one ear,

we will begin our story

with the word *and*

    (lines 42–45)

A continuation, a going forth. No punctuation. No end-stop needed. Ever.

Grand Rapids, Michigan

Note

1.   I referenced the low-residency MFA program at Goddard College in Vermont, which was founded in 1976 by poet Ellen Bryant Voigt. I attended the program from 1977 to 1979 and there met Lisel Mueller, who was my mentor and faculty advisor. I worked with her for my first semester (when I did the intensive research on fairy tales, folk tales, and myth) and my second semester (when I did major critical work and completed my MFA thesis on the seminal German poet Rainer Maria Rilke). Mueller was a significant advisor for those semesters and a pivotal member of my MFA team. In the early 1980s, Goddard College was having financial difficulties. Because of these factors, Voigt decided to move the MFA program—faculty, students, and curriculum—to Warren Wilson College in North Carolina, where it still resides today. In many ways, Warren Wilson is my alma mater. Goddard College developed its own MFA program years after Voigt's decision, but it wasn't the same program that I graduated from. In the spring of 2024, Goddard College in Plainfield, Vermont, closed permanently, citing shrinking enrollment and mounting financial challenges. In late July 2024, I went to Goddard's campus before the college shut down to obtain the original copy of my MFA thesis from their Pratt Library, where it was archived. As I walked through the campus one last time, I remembered meeting Mueller for the first time. And what an amazing time that was—and still is.

Works Cited

Gibbons, Reginald. Induction ceremony brochure. Chicago Literary Hall of Fame: Lisel Mueller, Era Bell Thompson, and Harry Mark Petrakis, The Poetry Foundation, 19 May 2022.

Mueller, Lisel. "Why We Tell Stories." *Alive Together: New and Selected Poems,* Louisiana State UP, 1996, pp. 150–51.

WHAT IS MIDWESTERN ABOUT THE POETRY OF LISEL MUELLER?

Janet Ruth Heller

In the third volume of *MidAmerica* (1976), David D. Anderson published an article entitled "Notes Toward a Definition of the Mind of the Midwest." He points out that many individuals have immigrated to the Midwest from Europe and from other areas of the United States (14). As a consequence, the Midwest "is simultaneously native and ethnic, nationalistic and conscious of origins" (15). In the conclusion of this article, Anderson summarizes the essential elements of the midwestern mindset. Although people who do not live in the Midwest have generated reductive stereotypes of the region, Anderson insists, "[T]he reality consists of variety, of unpredictability, of paradox, of a rejection of orthodoxy" (15–16). He emphasizes that the Midwest is "the heartland" of the United States (16).

Born in Hamburg, Germany, in 1924, Lisel Neumann immigrated to the United States in 1939 with her mother and sister. Her father, a historian and political dissident, had left Germany for the United States in 1937 after being arrested by the Gestapo ("Return: A Memoir" 38–39). Her parents, both teachers, settled in Evansville, Indiana, where her father taught French and German for Evansville College (now the University of Evansville). Lisel Mueller majored in sociology at Evansville College and met her classmate Paul Mueller there. In 1943, she married Paul Mueller, who worked as an editor, and in 1944, Lisel Mueller graduated from the University of Evansville. The couple built a home in rural Lake Forest, Illinois.

In this essay, I will focus on Lisel Mueller's book *Alive Together: New and Selected Poems* (1996), which won the Pulitzer Prize for poetry. In her poems, Mueller navigates between Europe and the United States, her past and her present, her national origin and her current status. She is fully aware of her environment in Illinois but also retains an interest in European history and culture. This dual consciousness pervades Mueller's poetry, and this duality is one source of her work's variety, complexity, and paradoxes. The poems in *Alive Together* often develop the theme of isolation but also rewrite European fairytales to express the problems of the modern world. Mueller challenges traditional ways of thinking and living with humanist and feminist critiques. She emphasizes the need to change to survive.

In a 1981 interview, Mueller told Stan Sanvel Rubin and William Heyen,

> I'm often asked if I consider myself a Midwestern poet, and my answer is yes and no.... [W]hen landscape appears in my poems it is a Midwestern landscape; I have lived almost continuously in the Midwest since my arrival, and my children were born and raised here.... I am more at home here than anywhere. At the same time I am not a native; I see the culture, and myself in it, through a scrim, with European eyes, and my poetry accommodates a bias toward historical determinism, no doubt the burdensome heritage of a twentieth-century native German. ("'The Steady Interior Hum'" 65)

Mueller published an essay in 1971 that attempts to define midwestern poetry, "Midwestern Poetry: Goodbye to All That." In his article "Lisel Mueller and the Idea of Midwestern Poetry" (1978), Paul Solyn comments on Mueller's definition of midwestern poetry. He agrees with Mueller that midwestern writing has tended to be realistic, that it uses simple diction, and that free verse predominates. Mueller and Solyn contend that the plain language and free verse result from "the informal, egalitarian heritage" of the region (Solyn 71–72). Mueller writes, "Free verse, Midwest style, was not a European import, but rather an introduction of everyday common speech patterns into the province of poetry" (7).

For similar reasons, midwestern poets are "not ... especially interested in poetic technique" (Solyn 72). Mueller writes,

Verbal innovation has never made real headway here, and elegance of style has neither been a goal nor a fact. In the old battle between virtuosity and integrity of feeling … Midwestern poets believe that the exposed grain of experience is far more beautiful than any glossy finish. ("Midwestern Poetry" 7)

Commenting on her own poetic style in an interview with Nancy Bunge, Mueller emphasizes, "I usually use strong, short words and not many latinates because they sound weaker to me." Since she prefers to discuss essential issues, what she terms "the elementary," Mueller chooses "strongly accented, strongly sounded Germanic words" ("An Interview with Lisel Mueller" 66). Mueller also read midwestern poets like Carl Sandburg, and their work influenced her poetic language ("Learning to Play by Ear" 34). Thus, her own diction reflects the influence of the midwestern ethos.

Solyn and Mueller also agree that midwestern writers emphasize individual people. Mueller insists, "This deeply ingrained humanism, this attention and respect accorded the individual person, may well be the special contribution of Midwestern poets to American poetry" ("Midwestern Poetry" 7). Edgar Lee Masters is a good example. Yet midwestern writers also emphasize people situated in a particular landscape (Solyn 74; Mueller, "Midwestern Poetry" 6).

Some poems in *Alive Together* specifically refer to the flora and fauna of the Midwest. "Cicadas" describes an insect that does not live in Germany but is abundant in the United States, including Illinois, where Mueller lived. Paradoxically, the poet refers to cicadas as "the rapt voice of silence" (*Alive Together*, hereafter AT, 58, line 2). Similarly, Mueller celebrates midwestern birds like "the purple finches, / the rusty blackbirds, / the ruby cardinals, / and the white-throated sparrows / with their liquid voices" (AT 39, lines 19–23) as her "guides" (line 13) in "Why I Need the Birds." The poet portrays birds and animals as guides in her other work also.

"Animals Are Entering Our Lives" traces the history of interactions between people and creatures. The poem begins with an epigraph from Jacob and Wilhelm Grimms' fairy tale "Little Brother and Little Sister," in which a young woman cares for her brother, who has been transformed into a deer by their evil step-mother, who is a witch. The sister puts her golden garter around the deer's neck to symbolize their bond. Remembering such folktales that emphasize closeness among species, Mueller imagines ancient times when humans and animals co-operated and "had a common language" (AT 37, line 7). Then, animals served as "guides and rescuers of the lost" (line 3). However, people began "to trample and plunder" the natural world (line 9). This caused alienation between humans and other species, who no longer spoke the same language (lines 11–14). Writing in the late twentieth century, Mueller insists that animals are now "coming back to us" (line 15). She gives examples of monkeys in Hong Kong but focuses on her own area of Lake Forest, Illinois, where "the gulls swarm over the parking lots" (line 25) and "Canada geese grow fat / on greasy leftover lunches / in the fastidious, landscaped ponds / of suburban corporations" (lines 27–30). She marvels that the birds now remain in Illinois all year round, departing from their custom of migrating south for the winter (lines 31–34).

In the conclusion to "Animals Are Entering Our Lives," Mueller returns to the image of interaction between deer and humans in her epigraph. She focuses on the deer who come to her family's garden every night "as if they had been in-vited" (AT 38, line 38). They eat "the tomatoes and tender beans, / the succulent day-lily blossoms / and dewy geranium heads" (lines 39–41) that her husband has planted. Mueller compares the deer to "refugees" (line 47), an image with resonance from the author's own life. The deer "refugees" are "defying guns and fences / and risking death on the road / to reach us, their dispossessors, / who have become their last chance" (lines 47–51). This passage emphasizes the iro-ny of the deers' dependency on human spoilers of the natural environment. The poet asks, "Shall we accept them again? / Shall we fit them with precious collars" like the sister in Grimms' folktale? (lines 52–53). People need to decide whether to live in harmony with nature again or to continue the centuries of hostility and mutual distrust. As in her other poems about the possibility of recovering the past, Mueller implies that humans should commit themselves to restoring the previous harmony, even if sacrifices like a ravaged garden are necessary.

Many of Mueller's poems concern snow, which Illinois and other midwestern states experience often. In "Not Only the Eskimos," Mueller contends that although non-Eskimos have fewer words for snow, we can distinguish different kinds of flakes in other ways. Using parallel clauses, the poet playfully creates new categories for snow, such as "guerrilla snow, which comes in the night / and changes the world by morning" (AT 124, lines 5–6) and "surreal snow in the Dakotas, / when you can't find your house, your street" (lines 11–12). Also, Mueller personifies the sun, which, after a blizzard, "licks black tree limbs, leaving us only one white stripe, / a replica of a skunk" (lines 15–18). Skunks are common in North America, but not in Europe.

The Midwest often receives what Mueller terms "unbelievable snows," such as blizzards in April, storms in early fall, and "the Big Snow on Mozart's birthday, when Chicago became the Elysian Fields / and strangers spoke to each other" (lines 19–24). Although blizzards can be a nuisance, they can also spur people to reach out to other suffering humans.

In "Figure for a Landscape," Mueller focuses on the landscape of a cold, silent midwestern winter day and "the solitary walker" who braves the elements. Both Germany and Illinois have harsh winters, and some of the Grimms' fairy tales portray characters sent out alone on a winter day by a cruel parent. For example, in "The Three Little Gnomes in the Forest," a jealous stepmother forces her beautiful stepdaughter out in the winter wearing only a paper dress, insisting that the girl bring home strawberries. Although the stepmother hopes that the youngster will freeze to death, the girl succeeds in her mission due to her kindness and the help of three gnomes whom she befriends.

Lake Michigan is a vast body of water that forms part of the northeastern boundary of Illinois. During warmer seasons, the lake attracts crowds of noisy hikers, swimmers, boaters, and sunbathers who gather on the shore and can hear the waves crashing on beaches and piers. Mueller emphasizes that, in contrast, this particular winter Sunday seems so quiet that "even the lake is petrified out of sound" ("Figure for a Landscape," AT 65, line 12).

Mueller perceives the solitary walker as heroic to venture out on the frigid, dangerous landscape:

> he is the hero who bears all loss,
> who, by no particular virtue
> other than solitude, takes on himself
> the full silence, the whole terrible
> knowledge the landscape no longer conceals. (lines 26–30)

Like the kind girl in Grimms' fairy tale, the solitary walker represents the best that humanity has to offer.

Lisel Mueller's poems often generate paradoxes to emphasize the complexity of the modern world. For example, "The Biographer" insists that such writers lose their own identity/individuality when they focus on the lives of other people. In the first stanza, Mueller compares a biographer to a surgeon who opens up the other person's life. In the second stanza, the poet portrays the biographer as consuming the subject's words like food. This second-hand language permeates the biographer's speech and breath. When the biographer follows "the journeys you took," he/she "walked in your tracks like a Chinese wife" (AT 80, lines 13–14). Eventually, the biographer moves into the home where the subject used to live and has "restored" the original décor. In the final lines of the poem, Mueller ironically imagines the subject returning and "asking / whose house this is" (lines 23–24). She implies that the biographer cannot completely take over a subject's identity.

Although the biographer has devoted his/her life to researching another person and fantasizes about having "eaten your heart" and turning into the subject, Mueller stresses that one cannot achieve full comprehension of another individual: "you slipped through your facts" (lines 16–18). Again, Mueller stresses the irony that full connection with and complete understanding of another human is impossible. Like the hiker in "Figure for a Landscape," the biographer remains solitary and lonely.

As part of Mueller's rejection of orthodoxy, she writes feminist poems. "Life of a Queen" draws many parallels between the lives of queen bees and the traditional lives of women. Early in the queen bee's life, the hive spoils her and workers "stuff her with sweets" (AT 82, line 4). This diet fattens the queen, but "Whenever she tries to stop eating / they open her mouth and force it down" (lines 11–12). This image emphasizes the vulnerable position of both queen bees and women: traditional society pampers them; however, they have no freedom of choice. When the queen has reached maturity, she mates briefly with a male bee. Then, her life is devoted to laying eggs. As the queen ages, she loses her value to the hive. Workers stop feeding her and devote their attention to her successor. The old queen starves to death while the newly crowned queen starts the cycle over again.

"Life of a Queen" emphasizes the boring and repetitive lives of many women, pushed to bear many children and then discarded by their society. Mueller implies that humans must break this exploitative cycle to progress and give women more varied and meaningful experiences.

Mueller's poems in *Alive Together* often concern important changes in societies and regions. "Place and Time" begins with a radio interview with a young man in North Dakota who explains that "the business district / of his hometown had been plowed under" (AT 7, lines 2–3) and is now covered with grass (lines 5–14). This midwestern town's crisis reminds Mueller of other historical calamities, such as "a buried Mayan temple / or a Roman aqueduct beneath / a remote sheep pasture / in the British Isles" (lines 19–22).

Using an image from Genesis, Mueller insists that all human beings suffer losses like those of the man in North Dakota. "We're all / pillars of salt," she writes (lines 33–34). Mueller herself feels like a pillar of salt because the rise of Nazism forced her family to flee from Germany. She recalls her mother playing Beethoven and Schubert on the family's Bechstein piano in Hamburg (7–8, lines 34–39).

Lisel Mueller's mother died young, and the family had to leave its piano in Germany, where it burned during World War II. However, whenever the poet hears a concert pianist, she imagines her mother playing the black Bechstein, and this memory restores "my prewar childhood city / intact and real" (8, lines 58–60). Lisel Mueller emphasizes that, similarly, some link enables the man from North Dakota to remember his town and retrieve its essence, "which does not change" (line 68).

"Losing My Sight" develops a related theme. As her vision deteriorates, the poet notices that her sense of hearing becomes more acute. She realizes that although birds make a lot of noise during the spring, they are "practically silent" in August (AT 10, lines 1–5). Furthermore, she can now distinguish between the different kinds of sounds that her local midwestern birds make: "screamers and whistlers and cooers / and O, the coloraturas" (lines 6–7). Personification emphasizes Mueller's new insights. Also, the poet hears pitch differences "in our cat's / elegant Chinese" (lines 9–10). As she struggles to see the local river, Mueller hears "its sighs and little smacks" (line 12). In addition, she can distinguish various noises of cars and trucks, and the sounds of nocturnal animals (lines 15–18). Crickets offer her "a continuous rope / of sound" (lines 20–21) that helps her navigate life.

A related poem, "Midwinter Notes," addresses aging and Mueller's loss of vision. She realizes that her photograph collection has more dead relatives and friends than living ones (AT 14, lines 1–2). She also observes that her pessimism and her husband's optimism balance one another: "Together we make the equinox" (lines 6–11). As usual, Mueller develops a paradox: while blindness makes her world "darker," "the sun / sends me sharper, harder / glances off glass, off ice— / like the white light reported / by the temporarily dead" (lines 12–17). Although she is aging, losing her sight, and moving toward death, a new kind of light illuminates her world.

"Midwinter Notes" develops another paradox: after most plants in her garden die, a beautiful lavender flower blooms (14–15, lines 26–32). Mueller sees this as "a brilliant contradiction / out of phase, like an angel / strayed into Time, our world" (15, lines 33–35). She ends this poem with another image of metamorphosis and resurrection:

At twilight, water in roadside ditches

pulls down the last light

to be transformed from lead

into softly gleaming silver.

It has taken me years to discover

this slant conjunction of sky and water

late in the day, when the dead

are allowed their brief shining. (15, lines 39–46)

This transformation and the new insights that arise as one ages are the themes of "Midwinter Notes."

Chicago, like New York, has been a center of activity for organized crime in the United States. In "Afterlife," Mueller dissects the way that people elevate mob bosses after their deaths. The process begins with "thousands" of mourners in the "funeral procession" (AT 29, lines 1–2). Mirroring the procedure for creating a new Catholic saint, people write hyperbolic songs, and legends spread about the dead criminal's precocity, generosity, and kindness. Like an earlier generation's deification of Jesus, followers report "sightings" of the dead criminal, who has allegedly risen from the dead. Forgetting the man's misdeeds, many people celebrate the "miracle" (line 17) of his air-brushed and cleansed life.

Americans consider the Midwest the central heartland of the United States. In her poem "Heartland," Mueller puns on the meaning of this word. She recalls William Wordsworth's sonnet "The World Is Too Much with Us," in which the English poet attacks the materialism of his era and contrasts it to earlier generations, which felt closer to nature. Mueller repeats Wordsworth's central image: "we've given our hearts away" ("Heartland," AT 30, line 1; "The World Is Too Much with Us," line 4). She considers her epoch a "heartless age" (line 23), despite its songs and protestations about the heart.

Lisel Mueller's poetry fits David D. Anderson's definition of the midwestern mindset. Her work is both deeply rooted in the American landscape and conscious of her German origins. Mueller's poems exhibit variety, unpredictability, paradox, and a rejection of orthodoxy. Her work also has the plain language, free verse, realism, and humanism that she sees as characteristic of the Midwest.

Michigan College English Association

Works Cited

Anderson, David D. "Notes Toward a Definition of the Mind of the Midwest." *MidAmerica*, vol. 3, 1976, pp. 7–16.

Grimm, Jacob, and Wilhelm Grimm. "Little Brother and Little Sister." *Kinder- und Hausmärchen* (*Children's and Household Tales—Grimms' Fairy Tales*), translated by D. L. Ashliman, 2001, sites.pitt.edu/~dash/grimm011.html.

Mueller, Lisel. *Alive Together: New and Selected Poems*. Louisiana State UP, 1996.

———. "An Interview with Lisel Mueller." With Nancy Bunge. *Learning to Play by Ear: Essays and Early Poems*, Juniper Press, 1990, pp. 66–74.

———. "Learning to Play by Ear." *Learning to Play by Ear: Essays and Early Poems*, Juniper Press, 1990, pp. 33–37.

———. "Midwestern Poetry: Goodbye to All That." *Voyages to the Inland Sea*, 1st ed., edited by John Judson, Center for Contemporary Poetry, University of Wisconsin-La Crosse, 1971, pp. 1–10.

———. "Return: A Memoir." *Learning to Play by Ear: Essays and Early Poems*, Juniper Press, 1990, pp. 38–45.

———. "'The Steady Interior Hum': A Conversation with Lisel Mueller." Interview with Stan Sanvel Rubin and William Heyen. *The Post-Confessionals: Conversations with American Poets of the Eighties*, edited by Earl G. Ingersoll, Judith Kitchen, and Stan Sanvel Rubin, Fairleigh Dickinson UP, 1989, pp. 65–72.

Solyn, Paul. "Lisel Mueller and the Idea of Midwestern Poetry." *Regionalism and the Female Imagination: A Collection of Essays*, edited Emily Toth, Human Sciences, 1985, pp. 67–80.

Wordsworth, William. "The World Is Too Much with Us." *Poetry Foundation*, www.poetryfoundation.org/poems/45564/the-world-is-too-much-with-us.

AN ALCHEMY OF WORDS
Lisel Mueller's "Monet Refuses the Operation"

Elizabeth Iannaci

> *Because each of us tells*
> *the same story*
> *but tells it differently*
> *—Lisel Mueller, "Why We Tell Stories"*

How anyone perceives anything is colored by and filtered through their experience, their knowledge, their sensibilities, and their eyes. In this manner, Voice and Vision are inextricably entwined. I don't know how far Lisel Mueller's glaucoma had progressed when she wrote "Monet Refuses the Operation," but I can't help but believe it was on her mind, that her condition, however advanced, informed the writing of this piece.

When I first encountered the poem in 2001, I had already been diagnosed with Retinitis Pigmentosa, a degenerative, hereditary disease for which there is still no treatment. I was slowly and irreversibly creeping toward a much smaller, dimmer world. A world at the end of a tunnel. A world in which I might have to, one day, "feel" my way to the bright side.

On rare occasions (not nearly often enough), a piece of writing has spoken to me so specifically that it's as though hands had reached out from the page, grabbed my lapels, and pulled me face-first into the text. Though my own experiences with cataracts wouldn't come for over a decade, I secured an instant affinity with Mueller's stunning work.

The poem is a persona piece in which Claude Monet refuses to have cataract surgery so that he can keep his artistic vision intact. At that time, my own deep-seated dread of impending blindness rendered me so immobile that this view of Monet's seeming handicap appeared downright radical. For an artist, to be altered by one's own physicality is anathema to the process, and a fate devoutly to be avoided. This is not unlike Barbra Streisand refusing to get her nose made smaller for the camera, or Freddie Mercury not having his overbite fixed, both vocalists fearing that the physical "correction" would damage the sound their "instruments" so spectacularly produced. Mueller's poem deals with vision in the same way.

I was unaware that Monet had developed cataracts and had, indeed, refused an operation to get them removed. His eyesight continued to diminish until he finally agreed to surgery in 1923. It was a painful and difficult undertaking for Monet, but ultimately successful, though the way he saw color was never quite the same. His vision improved enough, however, for him to disown work he'd done during his cataract period (1912–22). He eschewed the crude brushstrokes and gaudy colors. As a result, Monet destroyed or altered much of that work. Paintings that survived the destruction exist only because they were rescued by Monet's family or friends.

That an artist especially might find imperfect eyesight essential to their art was an astonishing and eye-opening supposition. Mueller's unique insight and understanding, however, prompted her brilliant opening lines:

> Doctor, you say there are no haloes
> around the streetlights in Paris
>
> …
>
> I tell you it has taken me all my life
> to arrive at the vision of gas lamps as angels, (lines 1–2, 5–6)

Yes, of course. On close examination, the poet makes it glaringly clear that what others view as a weakness the artist uses as a strength. What may sound like the ravings of a madman, rendered in oil by someone with incredible skill (or on paper—the right word in the right order), becomes a masterpiece.

Over the course of the poem, the tone moves from indignation and defiance to wonder and deference, ending in a near state of rapture. Nowhere in the piece is there any trace of regret over loss of sight. Neither is there the slightest hint of fear regarding blindness. Without any equivocation, the speaker refers to the way he saw things in the past as "my youthful errors" and does not mourn the clarity of vision that has changed. Evolved. Rather, it's a celebration of a unique viewpoint, arrived at over time. Arrived at only because of the artist's diminishing vision:

> Fifty-four years before I could see
> Rouen cathedral is built
> of parallel shafts of sun, (lines 12–14)

Mueller's expert use of the line-break after "before I could see" reinforces the idea of Monet's visual evolution, at the same time informing us that he now experiences the tangible and corporeal as vagaries of sunlight. The speaker has a pure and undeniable esteem for the oneness of the world, of how our perceptions of physical objects of every kind connect and relate to, then transcend that which borders or meets them. Thus, the artist is truly seeing things in a new and, from the speaker's point of view, a much truer way:

> the illusion of three-dimensional space,
> wisteria separate
> from the bridge it covers. (lines 18–20)

Most of us are familiar with Monet's painting of the bridge at Giverny, yet I can't recall a more accurate, yet succinct description of it. In fact, I am struck by Mueller's facility for complex description with a minimum of words, how few adjectives she uses—indeed, there is barely a handful in the entire poem. Still, the poet paints an almost fairy tale–like portrait of London's Parliament:

> the Houses of Parliament dissolve
> night after night to become
> the fluid dream of the Thames (lines 22–24)

There is an alchemy of words here—"dissolve" is the only verb, yet I can see movement, light dancing on the surface of the water. So economical, yet the description arguably rivals Monet's depiction in oil of those same structures. Mueller's clear voice throughout completely embodies the artistic and rebellious nature of the Impressionists. The artist's commitment is to Art. Art as the Artist sees it. The focus is on Light and how each artist has their own interpretation of the way light plays, reflects, and illuminates. The artist's vision cannot be compromised by what medicine, science, or society, for that matter, demand:

> I will not return to a universe
> of objects that don't know each other, (lines 25–26)

Though there is no mention of God or religion, there are references to haloes, angels, Rouen cathedral, and heaven. There is an implied relationship between art and the spiritual, especially where light is concerned. I can say from my own experience, cataracts can disperse light so that the world takes on an ethereal quality, as though I could see everything through a star-filter—edges are blurred, horizons fluid, colors almost malleable, even otherworldly:

> … light becomes what it touches
> …
> small fists passing sunlight
> …
> To paint the speed of light! (lines 29, 34, 38)

Here the poet uses the sole exclamation point. Is this not the essence of Poetry, to express the inexpressible, to describe the indescribable? How to paint the unpaintable is left to the reader. At this point, the poem has built a velocity that propels us forward toward the end, mixing with air to burn, transforming us into gases:

… Doctor,

if only you could see

…

… how infinitely the heart expands

to claim this world, blue vapor without end. (lines 42–43, 45–46)

Again, breaking the line after "if only you could see" urges us to see in a different way. To experience with an expanded heart. A heart dilated enough to give birth to the Infinite.

To take another look at the world and myself, illuminated by the light of this poem, was a revelation. It gave me an understanding of my own impending loss of vision I had not considered. It helped temper the dread I still felt at the time. I am deeply grateful for that.

I am a visual being. I remember things, not by hearing, but by seeing them. If something is important, I write it down. I won't need to refer to the note again. I'll remember because I "saw" it. So, it strikes me as one of the Higher Power's little chuckles that I'm losing my eyesight. My memory is a series of snapshots and film clips. As my vision continues to diminish, images become more precious. I'm drawn to filmmakers who have a unique visual style. Cinematographers are my heroes. Chiaroscuro and the play of light and dark capture my attention in all art forms. In fiction, I require an author who can "show" me their point. Raymond Chandler is a favorite because of his Noir imagery: "He stuck out like a tarantula on a wedding cake." (I dare you not to conjure a picture of that in your mind's eye.) I prefer poets who have a facility for creating image. Lisel Mueller is masterful at this. "Monet Refuses the Operation" is a poem about images. It unfolds as images. And perspective.

Mueller's Monet has a perspective uniquely his, peculiar only to him. He longs to share that aspect, that view, from his vantage point. Fortunately for us, Monet has Mueller to interpret, to show us what it might be like to see through his eyes.

When I was first diagnosed with RP, I was not yet 40 and still actively pursuing a career on the stage. The news devastated me. The theatre is no place for anyone partially sighted, actor or no. There were to be a couple of decades, as well as many close calls onstage and backstage, before my condition forced me to rethink my artistic life. I did the only smart and logical thing I could: I gave up acting for poetry! Poetry, I'd joke, because that's where the real money is. Even out-of-work actors laughed at that one. I had always written scenes, songs, plays, monologues. Now I write poems. I earned an MFA and was fortunate to study with some of the best poets alive.

Though I never had the opportunity to work with Lisel Mueller, I made it a point to study and know her work. The perception of each of us must filter through our own memoir, countless onionskin layers of life story, en route from trauma to ecstasy and back. Few have the talent, artistry, imagination, and insight to make their perception visible to others. Lisel Mueller did. No one else could have written "Monet Refuses the Operation." For me, this poem is an ars poetica-cum-magnum opus. An artist in possession of a rarefied vision, manifesting the unique viewpoint of another great artist. I don't think it gets any better than that. The poem is more than a testament to resilience; it's light years beyond making lemonade from the lemons given. It rather delivers a gourmet banquet of chrysanthemum-colored sunshine. And I gratefully bask in its glow.

Los Angeles, California

Works Cited and Referenced

Marmor, Michael F., and James G. Ravin. *The Artist's Eyes: Vision and the History of Art*. Abrams, 2009.

Mueller, Lisel. "Monet Refuses the Operation." *Alive Together: New and Selected Poems*, Louisiana State UP, 1996, pp. 186–87.

———. *Second Language*. Louisiana State UP, 1986.

———. "Why We Tell Stories." *Poetry Magazine*, July 1978, pp. 203–04.

ALIVE TOGETHER
Life and Language
with Lisel Mueller

Anita Skeen

In 1997, Lisel Mueller won the Pulitzer Prize for Poetry for her collection of new and selected poems, *Alive Together*. The collection reflected more than thirty-five years of the poet's writing life and addressed the issues so central to Mueller's life and work: history and culture, family, music, time and aging, art and language, and the seemingly insignificant moments that contain small or large epiphanies. When the book first came out and I had read the poems numerous times, I told my students that if I were stranded on a desert island, alone, for the rest of my life and could have only one book, I would choose *Alive Together*. More than twenty-five years later, I still feel the same way. In the dedication to the book, Mueller writes, "For my family; and for my former students, with gratitude for their friendship." How so like Mueller to be grateful to others for their friendship rather than acknowledging what she had given to us, particularly to her students.

I first met Lisel Mueller when I was a young assistant professor in the MFA program at Wichita State University and she came for a semester as our Writer in Residence. We'd had previous poets and fiction writers come to hold that position, and I'd enjoyed their company—but there was something about Mueller's quiet observation and intense curiosity that drew me to her almost instantly. My office was around the corner from her classroom, and several times I sat in on the small graduate poetry workshop she conducted. She was a teacher who taught by conversation, by providing a wealth of examples of excellent poems for the students to discuss, and by challenging students, through clever and thoughtful assignments, to write their own poems.

A decade and a half before this, when I was an English major at Concord College in Athens, West Virginia, I had a professor I consider to be my first mentor, Dr. James Shrewsbury, a Victorian literature scholar who conducted our small class on the novel sitting in one of the half-arm wooden chairs we all sat in, pulled into a circle so we could face one another. This was not how classrooms were set up in the late 1960s. He came to class with the book we were discussing and a cup of coffee. I never remember him reading from notes or lecturing us. We talked about the story, the characters, the themes, and the language. He asked questions, and we asked questions. It was in this class that I decided what to do with my life: I wanted to do what Dr. Shrewsbury did. And so I became a college professor who talked about books and ideas with interested students.

When I sat in on the classes that Mueller conducted while she was with us at WSU, I was so often reminded of Dr. Shrewsbury and why I was sitting there in the room with Mueller and the students. It was during this time that I came to consider Mueller as my second important mentor, both as teacher and writer. I have so often since then thought of the opening lines of her poem "Alive Together": "Speaking of marvels, I am alive / together with you when I might have been / alive with anyone under the sun" (lines 1–3). I was lucky to have been guided by Mueller through her teaching, her writing, and ultimately her friendship.

I would like in this essay to talk about several specific poems of Mueller's that I have carried with me since I first read them, ones that I have used in teaching and ones that have inspired my writing and touched my life. Since earlier I mentioned Mueller's gratitude to her former students, perhaps this is the time to highlight "Why We Tell Stories." Below the title of the poem, Mueller writes "For Linda Nemec Foster." When I moved from Kansas to Michigan, I met Linda and learned that she was one of Mueller's former students.

In more than fifty years of teaching, I have probably opened fifty percent of my classes with "Why We Tell Stories." "Because," the first word of the poem, sets the scene for the entire poem. We tell stories, and write poems, because, and she proceeds to give us some reasons why. So many of the concerns Mueller addresses in her writing are evidenced in this poem. The passing of time, our relationship to the natural world, the mystery of language, the history of our spiritual lives, our relationship to family, but above all, our need to tell the stories of our lives and the way those stories ultimately affect our lives.

A number of academics, most notably Christopher Booker, believe that there are only seven basic plots in all of storytelling, and we can find all seven throughout Mueller's work. In *Alive Together* and Mueller's other collections, we find those seven plots revealed in the stories she tells us of her own experience (voyage/return and rebirth); the characters in fairy tales she writes about (overcoming the monster and rags to riches); the historical characters and situations she reveals (comedy and tragedy); the mystery of individual lives, from her own daughters to Lot's wife to an Edward Hopper nude (the quest).

It has always been Mueller's precision with language—or as Samuel Coleridge put it, "the *best* words in the best order"—that has been so remarkable (qtd. in Coleridge 45, emphasis in original). Phrases like "silence is perhaps / the sound of spiders breathing / and roots mining the earth; / it may be asparagus heaving, / headfirst, into the light / and the long brown sound / of cracked cups, when it happens" ("What the Dog Perhaps Hears" lines 4–10). Or "My country was struck by history more deadly than / earthquakes or hurricanes" ("Curriculum Vitae" line 7). Or "the Russian snow we remember / along with the warmth and smell of our furs, / though we have never traveled / to Russia or worn furs" ("Not Only the Eskimos" lines 32–35). All those phrases transport us into the middle of the poem's experience because of their clarity of sensory detail and imaginative juxtaposition of images. Exquisite, poignant, and oh so precise.

But Mueller can be just as powerful and heart-stopping in short poems where the language is spare and the poem is tight, wound like a coil that springs when you reach the final lines. In one of my favorite poems, and one I use often in teaching, "Spell for a Traveler," Mueller casts a spell onto those of us who travel to such magical places as "the harbor of sleep" (line 1), "the city of chances" (line 3), "the palace of mirrors" (line 5), and "the fields of the dispossessed" (line 13). Having addressed the traveler multiple times, she concludes by asking us, "From the bay of forgetfulness come back with my name, / from the cave of despair come to me empty-handed, / from the strait of narrow escapes, come back, come back" (lines 16–18). Come back, come back, the unspoken plea in all our hearts when someone we love goes away from us.

I've thought of Mueller's poem "Whoever You Are: A Letter" in this same way. The tension builds line by line through the poem as we follow "Someone who does not know you ... Someone ... you see in the rearview mirror ... Someone climbing / a tower in Texas" (lines 1, 5–6, 9–10) until the final lines strike you like a bullet:

> Someone is already climbing
> a tower in Texas, is halfway up,
> is at the top, has sought you out
> and lifts his gun as though this death
> had anything to do with you. (lines 9–13)

This poem first appeared in *The Private Life*, the poetry selection for the 1975 Lamont Prize, published in 1976, ten years after Charles Whitman climbed to the observation deck at the University of Texas in Austin where he shot and killed fifteen people, injuring thirty-one others. At the time, this was the deadliest shooting by a lone gunman in US history.

I knew about this terrible event; it happened when I was an undergraduate student away in West Virginia. A few years later in Ohio, the poet I studied under as a graduate student in the MFA program at Bowling Green University was Fredrick Eckman, the father of Thomas Eckman, one of Whitman's young victims. My tangential relationship to Mueller's poem may have made her words that much more powerful for me. But this poem did very much have something to do with me when on February 13, 2023, at Michigan State University, Anthony Dwayne McRae killed three students and wounded five more, most of them in a classroom in Berkey Hall where many times I had taught creative writing classes. I thought how perfectly Mueller had captured the absolute randomness of such deaths, the fact that we have no connection to the killer—until we do. As children, we make up stories about killers and victims, but they remain distant from our everyday lives. Without Mueller's poem I might never have been able to articulate this awareness in my own poem on the subject, "How I Learned about Chaos Theory." Here are the final lines from that poem, one that uses as its epigraph Mueller's opening lines, "Someone is already climbing / a tower in Texas":

... Somewhere a man
in a winter jacket, handguns stuffed
into pockets, red shoes, loses himself
in a panicked crowd. His story is now
our story, one we did not make up, one
that has nothing to do with us. Until
it does. A few minutes. A lifetime. (lines 34–40)

Lisel Mueller understood both suffering and joy, how they form the particulars of our lives, and how though we all may be a part of a human community, we are alive with animals and birds and the natural world, communities in which we find great delight and connection. We also have our private lives, private moments, and private griefs. In her poem "About Suffering They Were Never Wrong," from *Second Language*, she pays tribute to and connects with W. H. Auden's famous poem "Musee de Beaux Arts," which begins with the lines, "About suffering they were never wrong, / The Old Masters: how well they understood / Its human position" (lines 1–3). Auden works his way through the tale of Icarus, as painted by Peter Brueghel, falling from the sky into the "green Water," where "the expensive delicate ship that must have seen / Something amazing, a boy falling out of the sky, / Had somewhere to get to and sailed calmly on" (lines 18–21). Our suffering is ours, and often ours alone, as the world goes on turning "Quite leisurely from the disaster" (line 15), unchanged and unaffected.

Back to Mueller's poem "About Suffering They Were Never Wrong": she recalls an incident of a woman "down the block" (our neighbor, or perhaps even friend) who hanged herself one day, noting how well those Old Masters understood "that the lives of other people / are as full of secrets / as the lives of spies" (lines 14–16). We think we know about our neighbors, what makes them tick, how their lives are normal and happy, when behind those lives, or underneath them, are losses and sorrows unnamed and unimagined; and those lives, the real ones, implode "one sunny afternoon / in October, a day so mild / the roses are tricked into blooming again" (lines 20–22).

Mueller's skill at bringing all the power and pain of Auden's poem into her poem by using as her title only six words from his first line is masterful. She may not be one of those Old Masters Auden refers to, but she is a master of painting her poem with a title that opens up her story with Auden's story and closes her story with an image of life continuing despite one person's loss.

Mueller shares with us her own suffering of how she came to write poetry. "It was soon after my mother died," she writes in "When I Am Asked," "a brilliant June day, / everything blooming … Nothing was black or broken / and not a leaf fell / and the sun blared endless commercials / for summer holidays" (lines 4–6, 12–15).

How many of us, writers of any genre, are often asked how we came to our craft, our profession? What was it that turned us to words rather than painting (Peter Brueghel) or music (Franz Schubert) or dance (Merce Cunningham)? Was there an epiphanic moment when we turned that corner or was there a long, perhaps winding road where we met Emily Dickinson and Walt Whitman, William Faulkner and Flannery O'Connor, Lorraine Hansberry and Edward Albee? Asked how she came to writing, Mueller answers, "I talk about the indifference of nature" (line 3). Remember Auden, how the ship sailed on past the boy fallen from the sky? It's the particulars of that indifferent natural world that stand out for her: "the gray stone bench" (line 16), "the lovingly planted garden" (line 8), "the pink and white impatiens" (line 18). Nothing was broken, no leaves were falling, and the sun paid no more attention to her loss than it did to the hubris of Icarus. Nothing around her acknowledged her grief. "I … placed my grief," she writes, "in the mouth of language, / the only thing that would grieve with me" (lines 16, 19–21).

I was writing poetry long before my mother passed away fifteen years ago, and I turned to poetry when she left me. I knew it would not be indifferent. And, as in Mueller's work in particular, poetry would manifest words and details and experience that I knew would grieve with me, language so skillfully laid down on the page that I found a pathway through sorrow. In a poem I wrote for Mueller in my first book, *Each Hand a Map*, I opened "Where We Are Going, Where We Have Been" with these lines: "We cannot say where our lives intersect, / yours and mine, myself and the pasts / that I am, the histories you are" (lines 1–3). It's clear to me all these years later that lives intersect here, on the page, in the experiences we share, the images we offer. "From the strait of narrow escapes," Mueller pleads, as do we, "come back, come back" ("Spell for a Traveler" line 18).

As an academic, I could not conclude this discussion of Mueller's work and her importance in my writing and my life without giving a nod to "Curriculum Vitae," one of my favorites of her poems and one I have used time and again in teaching. I'm reminded of Kentucky Poet Laureate George Ella Lyon's "Where I'm From," which has made its way around the world and back again several times. "I am from clothespins, / from Clorox, and carbon tetrachloride," says George Ella in opening her poem (lines 1–2). Mueller writes in "Curriculum Vitae," "1. I was born in a Free City, near the North Sea" (line 1). Look how much we know already. While George Ella's poem of four stanzas reveals the culture of her Appalachian childhood, Mueller's poem of twenty statements takes us from her birth to the writing of the poem.

Both poets address the circumstances of their upbringings and infuse their poems with a richness of detail, precision of language, and compact structure. I have had students in so many of my classes be moved by these two poems to tell us all about their backgrounds, their families, their fears, their losses. Mueller's life has more of the latter because it covers more years. "Curriculum Vitae" concludes with these two lines: "20. So far so good. The brilliant days and nights / are breathless in their hurry. We follow, you and I" (lines 39–40).

Though Mueller died in 2020, just before we lost so many people to COVID, she has not left us. She has given us words and poems to carry us through the dark times, to remind us of our past and make us hopeful for the future, to encourage us to see the usual in unusual ways. I will follow Mueller's words and poems, using them as touchstones while I go through those "brilliant days and nights" she speaks of. She will be alongside me on my journey, still.

Michigan State University

Works Cited

Auden, W. H. "Musee des Beaux Arts." *Chief Modern Poets of England and America*, 4th ed., The Macmillan Company, 1968, pp. I-363.

Booker, Christopher. *The Seven Basic Plots: Why We Tell Stories*. Bloomsbury, 2019.

Coleridge, Henry Nelson. *Specimens of the Table Talk of Samuel Taylor Coleridge*, 2nd ed. John Murray, 1836.

Lyon, George Ella. "Where I'm From." http://www.georgeellalyon.com/where. html.

Mueller, Lisel. "About Suffering They Were Never Wrong." *Second Language*, Louisiana State UP, 1986, p. 24.

———. "Alive Together." *Alive Together: New and Selected Poems*, Louisiana State UP, 1996, pp. 84–85.

———. "Curriculum Vitae." *Alive Together: New and Selected Poems*, Louisiana State UP, 1996, pp. 5–6.

———. "Not Only the Eskimos." *The Need to Hold Still*, Louisiana State UP, 1980, p. 24.

———. "Spell for a Traveler." *The Private Life*, Louisiana State UP, 1976, p. 18.

———. "What the Dog Perhaps Hears." *Alive Together: New and Selected Poems*, Louisiana State UP, 1996, p. 89.

———. "When I Am Asked." *Waving from Shore*, Louisiana State UP, 1989, p. 4.

———. "Whoever You Are: A Letter." *The Private Life*, Louisiana State UP, 1976, p. 3.

———. "Why We Tell Stories." *The Need to Hold Still*, Louisiana State UP, 1980, p. 62.

Skeen, Anita. "How I Learned About Chaos Theory." Unpublished. Used by permission of the author.

———. "Where We Are Going, Where We Have Been." *Each Hand a Map*, Naiad Press, 1986.

A WORD ABOUT LYRIC AND NARRATIVE IMPULSES IN THE WORK OF LISEL MUELLER

Elaine Terranova

What you can say about poetry: that it is a shuttling between narrative and lyric impulses. I want to look at how Lisel Mueller's poetry accommodates both and how she divides and amalgamates and shifts between them, and even gets on to something else entirely. In a half dozen volumes of poetry, beginning with *Dependencies* in 1965, Mueller tells the story of a life, the transition from one continent to another, old world to new, and the story of a marriage and family. In free verse, in crystal clear iambic pentameter. (In "Reasons for Numbers" she gives credit to the number 5, "For the invention of Milton and Shakespeare" [*Alive Together*, hereafter AT, 180, line 11].) Her figures are fresh and surprising but nail down the illusive world. From "The Concert": "The piano believes in nothing / and grins from ear to ear" (AT 100, lines 5–6). Paradox, personification, assonance, and a visual proof, QED, in such a concise take that it makes us trust her implicitly. Mueller's poetic voice is frank, clear, accessible; at the same time, considered, intelligent. Playful, yet authoritative; universal and also personal.

We think of personal expression as characteristic of lyric poetry. Wordsworth in fact called "all good poetry … the spontaneous overflow of powerful feelings" (xiv). It is the moment caught and held. If narrative is the journey, an order of events, calling attention to their duration or frequency, lyric is the end of the journey, the epiphany. It relates the tension between opposites, hope and fear, good and evil, light and dark. In Mueller's lyrics we sense that examination of feelings as if they were physical objects we could hold in our hands. It's an intimate and immediate kind of knowing she expresses that could be contrasted with the more narrative impetus of pursuit of an ending.

Language of course is the foundation for these messages, the ongoing and the caught short. And Mueller makes clear her reliance and awe at the power and flexibility of her adopted language, English. *Second Language* (hereafter SL) is in fact the title of one of her collections. She describes her relationship with English in *Learning to Play by Ear: Essays and Early Poems*: "For someone like myself … the second language assumes and retains a special fascination" (46). I remember my own presumption in a conversation with Mueller, characterizing English as somehow inferior to other European languages, less precise than German, less melodious than Italian or French, and her objection: "How can you say that? English has cognates, alternatives, so many possibilities, shorter words that allow so much flexibility." And so the basis of her poetry is not the speech she grew up with, but the new language, playing with its order, delighting in its puns, appreciating its seemingly infinite variability.

But Mueller never abandoned her native German as a literary language. She is translator of the Austrian poet and fiction writer Marie Luise Kaschnitz. In *Learning to Play by Ear*, Mueller likens the words a translator decides on to the choices a new speaker of English makes. She goes to a poem of Kaschnitz for the word *Länder* and weighs lands against countries, for *Meere*, pits seas against oceans. Mueller, always aware of the range of possibilities in English, perhaps brings this doublethink unconsciously into her own poems. "Obviously," she asserts, "sound, including weight, is, to a poet, as much a factor as sense in word selection" ("Introduction" x).

She alludes to "Kaschnitz's lyrical imagination and slow, painful self-discovery" in her introduction to the *Selected Later Poems* (x). In the same introduction, she divides the work according to the "prose-like syntax and long lines" of Kaschnitz's narrative poems and the "sparse, abrupt … unpunctuated manner of her lyrics" (x). The division between narrative and lyric is not so easy to pinpoint in Mueller's own poetry. Although she does use the short line in long, skinny poems like "A Short History of the Rose" (AT) and "The Need to Hold Still" (AT), much lyrical, song-like work has longer lines and plenty of punctuation: "Spell for a Traveler," in *The Private Life* (hereafter PL), for instance, where anaphora creates a music. "From" is repeated, the traveler's starting point, in line after line among the deconstructed narrative:

From the harbor of sleep bring me the milk of childhood,

from the ocean of silence bring me a grain of salt,

from the city of chances bring me my lucky number (PL 18)

A volume of Kaschnitz's stories, *Circe's Mountain*, includes a story well-known in Mueller's translation, called "The Fat Girl." This is a good illustration of Kaschnitz's preoccupation with parapsychology, the uncanny. The author encounters her early self as a child she wants to protect and nurture. The uncanny is a feature also of fairy and folk tales, an important influence on Mueller's work, another link she finds to her first language.

Lyric poems of Mueller's like "Second Sight" (SL) and "After Whistler" (SL) relate a kind of seeing through surfaces to another dimension, call it the uncanny, something that matches and surpasses daily life. Moon rather than sun, for instance, leads those mysterious young girls astray in "After Whistler," or at least on their own way: "When the other children / line up on the side of the sun, / they will choose the moon, / that precious aberration" (SL 18, lines 4–7). The moon, the imagination, throws a new light on things, increasing their value. The sun, allied with everything under it, that sequence of then, after, now, a direction that can be followed like the path of a story. The moon, the lyric impulse, bypasses the familiar, goes to the essence.

In her lyrics Mueller examines this other side of things, their undreamed of uses. Both "Paper-White Narcissus" (AT) and "Monarchs" (PL) describe the double nature of the word for which they are named. "Paper White" is the story of Narcissus, the green stalks closing over his manifold reflection, and "they are blind" (AT 13, line 16). Kings transform into butterflies in "Monarchs," both splendid, both transient. Using metaphors from the Grimms' tales and folk tales, pieces of narrative are flung in our path. They lead the reader on, the crumbs to her own slanting stories. Always, these bridges she has to the other world, moonlight, what's behind the mirror. "Mushrooms" (SL) is a lyric with a fixed, extended simile. "Pale aliens," she calls mushrooms, "sleepwalkers" (36, II, lines 3, 4). They have come like new immigrants, from the other side, the other side of life, in the yard, overnight, under the light of the moon. And consider this from the little succinct narratives of the poem, "Your Tired, Your Poor," which relates the journey of the new American: "Then you see that the moon / has chosen to follow you here" (AT 162, lines 35–36). The moon is always looking over your shoulder even while the sun is beckoning you on.

What should we say is the difference then between lyric and narrative, in Mueller's or any poetry? Well, it's easier to find the answer to that daunting question, "What's the poem about?" in a narrative. And even in a lyric, narrative gives a context for the expression of feeling. The lyric is most usually embedded in narrative, which tells us where we are when the song begins. Also, generally but not always, a narrative will have more connectives or will activate some in the reader's mind. It will start with "First" or "Once" and go on in a sequential manner and lead someplace. In dozens of poems, such as "Why We Tell Stories" (*The Need to Hold Still*, hereafter NHS) and "Reading the Brothers Grimm to Jenny" (PL), Mueller plays with the narrative form, and especially in "Palindrome" (PL), a backward chronology, where the narrator gets younger in each line: she's seeing without glasses, falling in love easily, wanting to read *Crime and Punishment*, willing herself not to get sick on a rollercoaster. A life is a narrative, and Mueller has given us "The Triumph of Life: Mary Shelley" (NHS), a persona poem that tells the story of the author of *Frankenstein*, wife of the poet Shelley. A long poem for Mueller, with eight parts, it is an affecting portrait that characterizes the heroine as one of those moon-driven girls with a lyric nature.

There's another kind of poem Mueller writes that cannot be configured as either lyric or narrative exactly. It evokes a different sensibility, historical or philosophical. It shares a world view with major European poets like Cavafy or Szymborska more than with contemporary American poets, a point of view that might be considered political. I am thinking of "Small Poem about the Hounds and the Hares" (PL) and "New Year's" (SL). In "New Year's" we find a tyrannical colonel and a suffering political prisoner, as we might in so many present-day nations. We are at dead winter, the darkest time of the year, and nature mimics our assertive gesture, our bravery. But nature is a fragile protector: Like glass, "the sky behind them / that handblown mauve and pearl / left from a gentler century" (SL 11, lines 18–20). If it shattered, we would "walk right into darkness," the darkness presaged from the rising and falling crow at the start of the poem (SL 1, line 23). And in "What Will You Do," that succinct history of the world, we are asked to consider, "What did you do … / when you were cheated of your fur / your prehensile tail … when the sun / stopped revolving around you / when animals started to disappear" (NHS lines 7, 9–10, 14–16).

And this is now, even later. It's a time when the sun has withdrawn, leaving us to our own devices, to use the imagination, rely on the surprising sanity of fairy tales, follow our own way to prescience by the light of the moon.

Philadelphia, Pennsylvania

Works Cited

Kaschnitz, Marie Luise. *Circe's Mountain: Stories by Marie Luise Kaschnitz.* Translated by Lisel Mueller, Milkweed, 1990.

Mueller, Lisel. *Alive Together: New and Selected Poems.* Louisiana State UP, 1996.

———. "Introduction." *Selected Later Poems of Marie Luise Kaschnitz*, translated by Lisel Mueller, Princeton UP, 1980.

———. *Learning to Play by Ear: Essays and Early Poems.* Juniper Press, 1990.

———. *The Need to Hold Still.* Louisiana State UP, 1980.

———. *The Private Life.* Louisiana State UP, 1976.

———. *Second Language.* Louisiana State UP, 1986.

Wordsworth, William. Preface. *Lyrical Ballads*, vol. 1., T. N. Longman and C. Rees, 1800.

WHILE "FATHER WAS BUSY ELUDING THE MONSTERS"

Jenny Mueller

When Lisel Mueller died in 2020, several obituaries noted the origin story of her art, as she herself had told it in "When I Am Asked." That poem describes how "the indifference of nature"—a blooming garden in June—gave no hearing to her sorrow over her mother's recent death. Thus she "placed my grief / in the mouth of language, / the only thing that would grieve with me" (*Alive Together*, hereafter AT, 198, lines 3, 19–21). This was the birth of her serious writing and her response, "When [she was] asked," to her readers who had questions about how she became a poet (line 1).

The poem is among her best known. It is immediately accessible, "grieving with" the poet while revealing almost nothing about Mueller's mother, Ilse Burmester Neumann, whose death at 53 was unmarked by the "brilliant June day" (line 5). The immediate cause of her unexpected, early death was a diabetes-related heart attack. However, Mueller and her father, Fritz Neumann, always believed that it was accelerated by the stress of years raising her daughters alone in Nazi Germany while Fritz Neumann was abroad, searching for work and evading arrest, "busy eluding the monsters" of European fascism that were spreading from home ("Curriculum Vitae," AT 5, line 8).

Such background is left out of "When I Am Asked" as an artistic choice that broadens its immediacy, of course. However, it also reflects a tension in Mueller's work: between poems that deal openly with her memories of childhood under Hitler and her experiences as a refugee, such as "Curriculum Vitae," and poems in which the force of this history exerts strong, but covert, pressure on seemingly unrelated work dealing with her settled life in the Midwest. The tension is partly imposed by an American readership that understood little of German history, and partly by her own need, as a refugee, to preserve her memories of a totalitarian state without reactivating its traumas. As she notes in "Virtuosi" (written during the same period as "When I Am Asked"), "People whose lives have been shaped / by history—and it is always tragic— / do not want to talk about it" (AT 206, lines 1–3). Yet the poetic voice that emerged in the garden after her mother's death could not stop talking about the history that marked her childhood and the lives of her parents, the refugee "Virtuosi" of the poem. She identified this history as her distinguishing theme.

Despite the national recognition her writing eventually gained, Mueller felt herself to be something of an outlier in American poetry.[1] Her European childhood inflected her thinking about the American lyric of her time and its frequent assumption of an apparently ahistorical personal voice. As she told an interviewer in 1993, "In Europe no one has had a private life not affected by history. I'm constantly aware of how privileged we (Americans) are" (qtd. in DeBrulye Cruze). In 1992, she pasted into her journal a portion of a book review concerning a collection of essays by the Polish émigré Czesław Miłosz. The last paragraph of the pasted text asserts that for Miłosz, "The divergence between European and American poetry ... presents itself as a conflict between their primary subjects: man in relation to history, or man in relation to Nature" (Kovaly; qtd. in Mueller's journal). Beside this, Mueller noted in the margin, "Exactly what I feel; how I see the difference." On the journal's next page, she added, "My preoccupation with history marks me as outside the mainstream of American poetry. No matter how long I've lived and written here, that has not changed and will not change."

Yet she was American and, as a midwesterner, squarely within a perceived mainstream. On the Poetry Foundation's Lisel Mueller webpage, her work is neatly compartmentalized for readers: one paragraph is devoted to history as her subject, another highlights that her work has "also been praised for its attentiveness to quiet moments of domestic drama, and its ability to speak to the experiences of family and semi-rural life" ("Lisel Mueller"). The transitional also splits the two themes discretely into nearly equal paragraphs, reinforcing a perception of binary emphases—first the poet's relation to history, then the poet's relation to a private "semi-rural life"—where Mueller herself saw a continual "preoccupation with history." In fact, her depictions of domestic, suburban American life are often made provisional, unsettled by memory. Images of flight, silencing, and evasion prove constant in her work, even that which presents a "domestic" face, speaking indirectly of the German past.

When she arrived in the United States in 1939 as a teenager, she was anxious to turn away from her history and fit in with her peers. After high school, college, and graduate school in Indiana, she moved to Illinois, settling into the house north of Chicago where she raised her American children and wrote all but one of her books. Yet, in a 1981 interview, she deflected a question as to whether she considered herself a midwestern poet, answering, "Let me say what countless other displaced persons must have said: I am more at home here than anywhere" (Interview with Rubin and Heyen 65).

"America saved me," she begins one poem, and so did pure luck (AT 88). But it could also be said that chances were made by the conscience of her father, Fritz C. Neumann. In the 1920s, Neumann was a secondary schoolteacher in Hamburg. He was part of Germany's "reform pedagogy" movement—similar in some ways to progressive education in the United States, but with a more radical social mission. For several years he taught at Hamburg's Lichtwark School, which became well known for its encouragement of reformist experimentation among teachers and pupils. The Lichtwark also gained a "red" reputation, pushed by its Marxist-leaning faculty, including Neumann. By 1930 there came an inevitable reaction, and Neumann's known politics led to his transfer to another Hamburg school. In 1932, after privately offering a lecture on Marx for an adult Workers School, of which he was then chair, he was arrested and charged with high treason. He was freed due to a general amnesty for political prisoners during the upheavals of that critical year, but with Hitler's ascendance to chancellor in 1933, he was banned from secondary school teaching under the new Nazi "law to restore the civil service." The law prohibited Jews and politically suspicious persons—including known anti-Nazis such as Neumann—from numerous positions, including teaching. He was out of work (Neumann, "Memoirs" 108–67).[2]

This turn of events led to a long period of separation from his wife and two daughters, setting in motion a lifelong pattern of migration, as Neumann eked out poorly paid, temporary teaching positions and sought work during the Depression in France, England, and Italy. In most cases this work involved teaching the children of German Jews or of other political refugees, learning in private, provisional boarding schools where they could study safely outside of Germany, and where their faculty could safely teach. At times Neumann quietly returned to take work in Hamburg, including private tutoring of Jewish children. But such periods were brief and largely ended after 1935, when Neumann paid a visit to the home of another dismissed schoolteacher who, unbeknownst to him, was also using her apartment as a meeting place for a resistance group.[3] Neumann was arrested and held in the Fuhlsbüttel concentration camp outside Hamburg. After questioning, he was luckily released, but it was clear he was not safe in Germany and he spent the next two years mainly in Italy, while his wife struggled to support their two children alone. In 1937, while Neumann was teaching in a school for German Jews in Italy, a Lichtwark School connection recommended him for a scholarship at the Graduate Teachers College in Illinois. He emigrated to the United States and was eventually offered college teaching positions in Illinois and Evansville, Indiana, allowing him finally to reunite with his family in 1939 (Neumann, "Memoirs" 168–209). His wife and daughters sailed to the United States shortly before World War II. Lisel Mueller became a midwesterner.

She did not travel back to visit Germany until 1983. Her brief published prose memoir about that trip, called "Return," describes how she felt a need finally to "come face to face with [her] childhood" after her father's death (*Learning to Play by Ear*, hereafter LPE, 38). This meant confronting "the bad memories of the terror we lived in under the Third Reich, where you could disappear for not giving the Hitler salute, for a disparaging remark about the government," and where her father's whereabouts needed to be kept secret (38). However, her poems generally place her childhood's "whole atmosphere of terror and necessary secrecy" in the background, or they leave it unmentioned (Interview with Karla Hammond 146). There are several reasons for this. Her feelings about American confessionalism were decidedly mixed. She got bored writing about herself and often turned to personae, whose voices indirectly process past trauma and express the urgency of truthful—if often unheard—testimony. As a non-Jewish survivor of the Nazis, she was conscious that her immediate family's sufferings in no way compared with the Holocaust, nor with the pain inflicted by Allied firebombings that affected others left behind, including her Hamburg friends and grandparents. In addition, her own testimony was likely to be poorly understood—even today, few grasp the concept of a German political refugee. (I think this must have been a cruel fact of her American life, since it would have once again suppressed her father's story.) But perhaps most important, and as she herself noted in a poem, her own memory was "selective," emphasizing "highlights" that were "all I can bear / of a painful childhood" ("Beginning in 1914," AT 117, lines 48, 50–51).

"Cavalleria Rusticana," for example, starts with a description of her "semi-rural" Illinois home on summer evenings. There, "All the fireflies in the world / are gathered in our backyard," their lights pulsing to the heated "scraping" of cicadas, noising "like country fiddlers," though with a "minimalist" tune (AT 200, lines 1–2, 8, 10, 13). She then turns to an isolated highlight from childhood:

As a child
one summer night in Verona
at my first opera,
I watched a swarm of matches
light up the Roman arena
until we were silent. It was as if
music were a night-blooming flower
that would not open
until we held our breath.
Then the full-blown sound,
the single-minded combat
of passion: voices sharpening

their glittering blades on one another,

electing to live or die. (lines 16–29)

Left out, to single out this moment of beauty, is the memory's larger context of danger, of displaced persons "eluding the monsters." In 1935, her father was recommended for a teaching appointment at a newly opened school in Gardone Riviera, Italy, for German Jewish children, known by its residents as the "Villa Jacobi" after its founder, who also owned its premises. He lost this chance while he was held for questioning in Fühlsbuttel (although he was attempting to recruit additional faculty for the Villa Jacobi when he was arrested). However, upon release he arranged with Frau Jacobi to lead a group of Jewish children privately on a monthlong summer field trip to Gardone from Hamburg, taking along his wife and eldest daughter, Lisel. During this trip he sought other teaching in Italy (eventually returning to the Villa Jacobi as faculty in 1937). Thus, the adults must have been anxious. The Villa Jacobi's location was idyllic, but it could shelter its residents only temporarily. Down the road lived a neighbor of poisonous fame: the proto-fascist, mob-rousing war hero and poet Gabriele D'Annunzio. Nazi officials frequented the local hotels, and most Italians had embraced fascism. Among the Villa Jacobi's Jewish students, and thus probably also at the opera, was Lisel Mueller's first love, whom she described in a short, never published written recollection of the trip:

> In Italy I fell in love … The object was a boy a year older than I, a boarder at Villa Jacobi, whose dark eyes and hair, coupled with his soft features, fired the romantic heart of the blond, blue-eyed child I was. I still have a picture of him which I took on the Plaza San Marco in Venice … I wonder what became of him, whether he survived the Holocaust, whether his family emigrated to another country. (Unpublished journal)

Mueller's papers also include a handwritten, fragmentary prose draft, never published but saved for decades, on pages brown with time. They suggest the slow process by which more terrifying images from childhood entered her work. A section titled "How It Was: 1938" begins thus:

> There is a public service announcement on television, harmless enough for most, which threatens me. "Open your mind: read," it says to the school-age children, bringing them in quick succession a sampler: a few book jackets, a few phrases, a few sound effects. The sound that threatens me comes between the annals of medicine and the romance of the cowboy; it is a low, guttural sound, indeterminate [inarticulate][4] as thunder: the *Sieg Heil* of my childhood.
>
> Twenty-eight years, how unimaginably slow is the speed of that sound, the sound that is still out to get me, just as it was on those Sunday afternoons before my grandmother's radio, when the hysterical voice ranted on for two hours, and the low-in-the-throat thunder which interrupted it, that huge communal gullet, was always on the edge of breaking out wild and swallowing me alive.
>
> Twenty-eight years and I stiffen: … I am a serious, unsmiling girl again, a touch-me-not wired with too many secrets.

"Twenty-eight years" suggests this writing was done in the 1960s, when her children were small and the public service announcement would have played on a black-and-white television kept in the basement "den." However, the "hysterical voice" was not allowed into her poetry until, at the earliest, the late 1970s, when her children were fully grown. Then, it appears in *The Need to Hold Still*'s autobiographical "Beginning in 1914," which imagines her life as a multi-reeled movie of fragments:

> The swastika
> appears and remains as the huge
> backdrop against which we're seen.

The sound track of a hysterical voice
is threatening us. We're heard as whispers. (AT 117, lines 51–55)

The need to whisper or hold silent was especially associated with her father. Elsewhere in "How It Was," she writes,

> During his periods at home with us, there was a sense of fear, of furtiveness, of submerged terror, as well as a desperate uncertainty about the future … Something threatening, something with fangs always behind you, something with claws on the other side of the door. Whispered rumors overheard, about a wife who received her husband's remains back from a concentration camp in a closed coffin … About the escapes and whereabouts of former students and friends of my father. The way my parents stiffened, the look in their eyes, if the doorbell rang late at night or unrecognized footsteps came up the stair.

The image of the withheld "claws" again waits to arrive in a poem, appearing in 1992 in the twenty-section "Curriculum Vitae." Section 3 reads, "Parents and grandparents hovered around me. The world I lived in had a soft voice and no claws." But by section 8, this world is obliterated: "My father was busy eluding the monsters. My mother told me the walls had ears. I learned the burden of secrets" (AT 5).

Washing back with the hysterical voice was "the fact that I could never, ever tell about my father—who he was, where he was; that I had to lie and evade to my schoolmates, I who was proud of him" ("How It Was"). But she remembers how much she had wanted to speak, to confide, to express. Keeping quiet drove her imaginative life deeper, perhaps setting the patterns of saying and silence that later surface in her poems. In the late 1970s she wrote in her journal about the importance of "*saying* [emphasis in original] … that I say the poem in my head, or sometimes softly out loud, [while] writing down those heard, said lines is a distraction," which "breaks that thread." She added,

I see now how far back that need to hear words in my own voice goes, re-membering how as a child I talked to myself, how, at 12, 13, 14, I would walk back from school with my lips clamped shut because the impulse to *articulate* my thoughts was overwhelming. (Unpublished journal)

During this time, she longed to be an actress. She later said that this early am-bition may have led to her fondness for poetic personae, and it is notable how often these voices—such as the solitary Venus speaking from the deserted beach in "Testimony"—open their lips to reveal a history that was previously secret, misinterpreted, unheard. Letters her father wrote to her from Italy show an on-going conversation about movies playing in Hamburg and Gardone. Lisel must also have written about her studies, since in 1937, Fritz Neumann responded,

I am very pleased that you have improved your knowledge of history. As you know, I have always been interested in history. Only an interest and study of history will give you the opportunity later on to understand in a deeper and more comprehensive sense the events that have now affected Europe and family life so much. From the outset, strive with all your might in this field for a view of things that is really so common to all … who are involved in historical events.

This historical view of things, which later became the feature by which Muel-ler identified herself as excluded from American poetry's mainstream, is also the burden of knowledge carried by her poetry's personae. Like the actress she wished to be, they often arrive in spare, level spaces that provide the poems' stag-es: Venus's deserted beach, Lot's wife looking back on Sodom in "Pillar of Salt" (as the Neumann family might have looked back on firebombed Hamburg, flat-tened by Operation Gomorrah), the unnamed speaker granted asylum in "Your Tired, Your Poor," who "stand[s] in the desert / heavy with what I smuggled in / behind my eyes and under my tongue: / memory and language" (AT 162, lines 10–13).

Fritz Neumann's incessant movement continued all his life. Arriving, tired and poor, in the Midwest in 1937, he gained a position in 1939 teaching languages at Indiana's Evansville College. (There, Lisel met and married Paul Mueller.) However, the longest of his several American academic positions was as a professor of history at Chicago's Roosevelt College. After Ilse Burmester's death, he returned to Hamburg, yet traveled back every year to visit the United States, often by ship. In his 70s, he came to live permanently with Mueller's family in Illinois. By this time he was suffering from aphasia and dementia, apparently the result of strokes. He rarely spoke. He spent his days pacing restlessly in the small house or in a living room armchair, placed beside a table full of books which at last he could not read—and which mainly concerned history, once the topic of his lectures. In "Bread and Apples," a 1980s poem about how "memory raises landmarks / unbidden," this is how he suddenly comes back: "My father sits / in the long-discarded chair; / the pages of the history book / he leafs through keep springing back / to the beginning" (AT 159, lines 14–20).

In her 1986 essay "Return," Mueller explains that

> my lonely father, who after [my mother's] death became a restless transcontinental traveler, has been dead seven years now. He had been the remaining link to my childhood, and his trips back and forth had given me the connection between here and there and at the same time spared me the pain, the conflicting feelings I thought I would have to confront if I myself went back [to Germany]. Now the connection is broken, and it is up to me to restore it. (LPE 38)

Neumann also becomes a connecting figure, "back and forth," between Mueller's seemingly "private" poems of Illinois life and those that deal explicitly with her German history. This can be seen in two poems in which he appears, but in strikingly different ways—"Voyager" and "Another Version."

Published in the same year as "Return," "Voyager" memorializes Neumann's restless movement, his gift for adaptation, his analytical and moral vision. Mueller imagines that in death he is still traveling on his favorite transport, the steam-ship, where she pictures him "looking through the eyeholes, / nearsighted and patient as always, / still knowing everything"—including the language of this new country's "boatmen in the black barges" (AT 157–58, lines 6–8, 10):

> No matter what bundle of time
> they inhabit, you will direct them,
> warn them once more and once more in vain
>
> You who changed countries more often than shoes
> can step ashore anywhere (lines 12–16)

But, as later lines in the poem reveal, this capable survivor was unable to bear the disaster of Ilse Burmester's death. In a cruel reverse of the imagery in "When I Am Asked," grief turns the poet's mourning father into an unlistening garden in "Voyager":

> Slowly you turned to stone
>
> And I, your daughter-keeper—
> what did I know about
> the sentience of stone?
> I watered you with indignities
> and tears, but you never bloomed. (lines 25–30)

"Voyager" also employs one of Mueller's favorite poetic allusions, expressing a central dilemma in her poems. Her description of a father "who changed countries more often than shoes" is a reference to Bertolt Brecht's poem "An die Nach-geborenen," whose title might be translated as "To Those Born Later" or "To Future Generations." Written in 1939, Brecht's poem speaks of the peripatetic lives of refugees from European fascism. He describes for later generations their search for security, "changing countries more often than shoes," and asks, "What times are these, when / it is almost a crime to talk about trees / because that means being silent about so much evil?" (Mueller, "On Reading" epigraph)—when expressing feeling for nature becomes an intolerable silence about history.

Mueller was aware that such "talking about trees" presented problems for the American lyric of her time, which often seemed to shut out the country's tumultuous social discord by seeking out muted, private epiphanies in nature. She struggled with this problem in her own work, and again quoted Brecht's lines on trees, silence, and evil in "Triage," a poem that also notes, "To speak of one thing is to suppress another. When I talk about myself, I cannot talk about you" (AT 217). This conclusion bears consequences for any poet who values accessibility, but particularly for the refugee poet in a country whose citizens live in privileged ignorance of history.

An earlier poem concerning the death of Felix Neumann is "Another Version," from *The Need to Hold Still* (hereafter NHS). Written during his last years when he lived with Mueller's family in Illinois, it is a poem about Mueller's midwestern home and her European history—but here, as so often in her work, the history is left unspoken. The poem's natural objects are her staples: snow, trees, the domesticated flora and fauna of the Illinois suburbs. Its people include refugees and displaced persons, but they are never named as such:

> Our trees are aspens, but people
> mistake them for birches;
> they think of us as characters
> in a Russian novel, Kitty and Levin
> living contentedly in the country.
> Our friends from the city watch the birds
> and rabbits feeding together
> on top of the deep, white snow.
>
> ...
>
> As in a Russian play, an old man

lives in our house, he is my father;

he lets go of life in such slow motion,

year after year, that the grief

is stuck inside me, a poisoned apple

that won't go up or down.

But like the three sisters, we rarely speak

of what keeps us awake at night;

like them, we complain about things

that don't really matter and talk

of our pleasures and of the future:

we tell each other the willows

are early this year, hazy with green. (NHS 5, lines 1–8, 12–24)

"Another Version" is exactly the kind of poem the Poetry Foundation means in describing "Mueller's work [that has] also been praised for its attentiveness to quiet moments of domestic drama, … family and semi-rural life" ("Lisel Mueller"). It does at first seem like an escape. Quite literally, it "talks about trees" while seeming to have little to do with historical evil. Requiring at most a passing knowledge of two classics of Russian literature, the poem is accessible to a casual reader who feels welcomed by its "universal" concerns of private family life. But I note that the poem begins in error—the aspens are not birches—and ends in secrecy, even as it presents a seemingly open face to its reader. Its theme is buried meaning.

Paradoxically, one of these buried meanings is the non-existence of the untouched private life. The slowly dying old man is Neumann, an ex-professor, victim, and survivor of history—though none of that is said. As in the German 1930s recalled in her journals and drafts, he is home with his daughter, but he continues to keep quiet, and she still cannot speak about him openly. She talks about trees, instead. Her poem makes the pain of such evasion its point.

The misunderstandings pile up. The friends from Chicago think they are arriving in the "country," even though by the time of the poem's composition, the rural character of this part of Illinois was almost gone. Nevertheless, the city guests sentimentalize the long-married Lisel and Paul as specimens of country family contentment, domestic Kitty and Levin, free of Anna and Vronsky's urbane torments (and, perhaps, of their narrative interest). The Chicago guests would have been looking through the modernist glass walls of a new living room, added by the Muellers to help house their increased family in the early 1970s, and gazing fondly through those walls at the feeding creatures on the Illinois snow.

Yet even that peaceable kingdom was never safe in Mueller's poetry, where the cries of wild animals tear her from sleep, and where the poet remade the family dog and the yard's rabbits into her "Small Poem About the Hounds and the Hares," a fable in which the hounds, "drunk on the blood of the hares," pause after the feast "to talk of how soft / were their pelts, how graceful their leaps, / how lovely their scared, gentle eyes" (AT 72, lines 4–7). This, too, is "another version" of Mueller's domestic pastoral—in which the poet gazed out at the midwestern scene and discovered, looking past the meek wildlife and deeper into the aspens, a view of history's terrors and the dangers of selective remembrance.

McKendree University

Notes

1. In this essay, I have excised the phrase "my mother" for the formality of an academic journal. I am the younger of Lisel and Paul Mueller's two daughters.

2. Neumann's memoirs are held by the German Historical Institute Washington (Washington, DC) and by Stanford's Hoover Institution. Titled "Memoirs of a Contemporary," they deal particularly with the turbulent politics of Germany in the 1920s and 1930s, in language reflecting Neumann's late career as a history professor. They end with Ilse Burmester's death, a loss from which he never fully recovered. An exhaustive German Wikipedia page on Neumann draws heavily from this text.

3. This was Hilde Schottlaender, later Hilde Marchwitza. The daughter of William Stern and sister of Günther Anders, she served two years in prison for

treason after the raid in which Neumann was also arrested, then fled to the United States after her release.

4.   Mueller's annotation inserts "inarticulate" as an alternate word choice.

Works Cited

DeBrulye Cruze, Karen. "Bringing It All Together." *Chicago Tribune*, 5 Dec. 1993, www.chicagotribune.com/news/ct-xpm-1993-12-05-9312050030-story.html. Accessed 27 Oct. 2023.

Kovaly, Heda. "The Seductive Banality of Life." *The New York Times*, 26 Apr. 1992, www.nytimes.com/1992/04/26/books/the-seductive-banality-of-life.html. Accessed 27 Oct. 2023.

"Lisel Mueller." *Poetry Foundation*, 2023, www.poetryfoundation.org/poets/lisel-mueller.

Mueller, Lisel. *Alive Together: New and Selected Poems*. Louisiana State UP, 1996.

———. "Another Version." *The Need to Hold Still*, Louisiana State UP, 1980, p. 5.

———. "How It Was: 1938." Unpublished and undated manuscript. Personal collection of Jenny Mueller.

———. Interview with Karla Hammond. *Chowder Review*, no. 10–11, 1978, pp. 146–56.

———. Interview with Stan Sanvel Rubin and William Heyen. *The Post-Confessionals: Conversations with American Poets of the Eighties*, edited by Earl G. Ingersoll et al., Fairleigh Dickinson UP, 1989, pp. 65–72.

———. *Learning to Play by Ear: Essays and Early Poems*. Juniper Press, 1990.

———. "On Reading an Anthology of Postwar German Poetry." *The Private Life*, Louisiana State UP, 1975, p. 24.

———. Unpublished journal. Personal collection of Jenny Mueller.

Neumann, Fritz C. Letter to Elizabeth Neumann [Lisel Mueller]. 30 March 1937. Personal collection of Jenny Mueller.

———. "Memoirs of a Contemporary." Unpublished typescript. 1965. Hoover Institution Library & Archives.

The following poems are reprinted by permission of Louisiana State University Press from *Alive Together: New and Selected Poems* by Lisel Mueller. Copyright 1996 by Lisel Mueller.

I also want to express my deep appreciation to Jenny Mueller, the literary executor of Lisel Mueller's estate, for her invaluable assistance in securing these rights.

—*Linda Nemec Foster*

CURRICULUM VITAE
1992

1) I was born in a Free City, near the North Sea.

2) In the year of my birth, money was shredded into confetti. A loaf of bread cost a million marks. Of course I do not remember this.

3) Parents and grandparents hovered around me. The world I lived in had a soft voice and no claws.

4) A cornucopia filled with treats took me into a building with bells. A wide-bosomed teacher took me in.

5) At home the bookshelves connected heaven and earth.

6) On Sundays the city child waded through pinecones and primrose marshes, a short train ride away.

7) My country was struck by history more deadly than earthquakes or hurricanes.

8) My father was busy eluding the monsters. My mother told me the walls had ears. I learned the burden of secrets.

9) I moved into the too bright days, the too dark nights of adolescence.

10) Two parents, two daughters, we followed the sun and the moon across the ocean. My grandparents stayed behind in darkness.

11) In the new language everyone spoke too fast. Eventually I caught up with them.

12) When I met you, the new language became the language of love.

13) The death of the mother hurt the daughter into poetry. The daughter became a mother of daughters.

14) Ordinary life: the plenty and thick of it. Knots tying threads to everywhere. The past pushed away, the future left unimagined for the sake of the glorious, difficult, passionate present.

15) Years and years of this.

16) The children no longer children. An old man's pain, an old man's loneliness.

17) And then my father too disappeared.

18) I tried to go home again. I stood at the door to my childhood, but it was closed to the public.

19) One day, on a crowded elevator, everyone's face was younger than mine.

20) So far, so good. The brilliant days and nights are breathless in their hurry. We follow, you and I.

THE BLIND LEADING
THE BLIND

Take my hand. There are two of us in this cave.
The sound you hear is water; you will hear it forever.
The ground you walk on is rock. I have been here before.
People come here to be born, to discover, to kiss,
to dream, and to dig and to kill. Watch for the mud.
Summer blows in with scent of horses and roses;
fall with the sound of sound breaking; winter shoves
its empty sleeve down the dark of your throat.
You will learn toads from diamonds, the fist from the palm,
love from the sweat of love, falling from flying.
There are a thousand turnoffs. I have been here before.
Once I fell off a precipice. Once I found gold.
Once I stumbled on murder, the thin parts of a girl.
Walk on, keep walking, there are axes above us.
Watch for occasional bits and bubbles of light—
birthdays for you, recognitions: *yourself, another*.
Watch for the mud. Listen for bells, for beggars.
Something with wings went crazy against my chest once.
There are two of us here. Touch me.

MOON FISHING

When the moon was full they came to the water,
some with pitchforks, some with rakes,
some with sieves and ladles,
and one with a silver cup.

And they fished till a traveler passed them and said,
"Fools,
to catch the moon you must let your women
spread their hair on the water—
even the wily moon will leap to that bobbing
net of shimmering threads,
gasp and flop till its silver scales
lie black and still at your feet."

And they fished with the hair of their women
till a traveler passed them and said,
"Fools,
do you think the moon is caught lightly,
with glitter and silk threads?
You must cut out your hearts and bait your hooks
with those dark animals;
what matter you lose your hearts to reel in your dream?"

And they fished with their tight, hot hearts
till a traveler passed them and said,
"Fools,
what good is the moon to a heartless man?
Put back your hearts and get on your knees
and drink as you never have,

until your throats are coated with silver
and your voices ring like bells."

And they fished with their lips and tongues
until the water was gone
and the moon had slipped away
in the soft, bottomless mud.

READING THE BROTHERS GRIMM
TO JENNY
Dead means somebody has to kiss you.

Jenny, your mind commands
kingdoms of black and white:
you shoulder the crow on your left,
the snowbird on your right;
for you the cinders part
and let the lentils through,
and noise falls into place
as screech or sweet roo-coo,
while in my own, real world
gray foxes and gray wolves
bargain eye to eye,
and the amazing dove
takes shelter under the wing
of the raven to keep dry.

Knowing that you must climb,
one day, the ancient tower
where disenchantment binds
the curls of innocence,
that you must live with power
and honor circumstance,
that choice is what comes true—
O, Jenny, pure in heart,
why do I lie to you?

Why do I read you tales
in which birds speak the truth

and pity cures the blind,
and beauty reaches deep
to prove a royal mind?
Death is a small mistake
there, where the kiss revives;
Jenny, we make just dreams
out of our unjust lives.

Still, when your truthful eyes,
your keen, attentive stare,
endow the vacuous slut
with royalty, when you match
her soul to her shimmering hair,
what can she do but rise
to your imagined throne?
And what can I, but see
beyond the world that is
when, faithful, you insist
I have the golden key—
and learn from you once more
the terror and the bliss,
the world as it might be?

ALIVE TOGETHER

Speaking of marvels, I am alive
together with you, when I might have been
alive with anyone under the sun,
when I might have been Abélard's woman
or the whore of a Renaissance pope
or a peasant wife with not enough food
and not enough love, with my children
dead of the plague. I might have slept
in an alcove next to the man
with the golden nose, who poked it
into the business of stars,
or sewn a starry flag
for a general with wooden teeth.
I might have been the exemplary Pocahontas
or a woman without a name
weeping in Master's bed
for my husband, exchanged for a mule,
my daughter, lost in a drunken bet.
I might have been stretched on a totem pole
to appease a vindictive god
or left, a useless girl-child,
to die on a cliff. I like to think
I might have been Mary Shelley
in love with a wrongheaded angel,
or Mary's friend. I might have been you.
This poem is endless, the odds against us are endless,
our chances of being alive together
statistically nonexistent;
still we have made it, alive in a time

when rationalists in square hats
and hatless Jehovah's Witnesses
agree it is almost over,
alive with our lively children
who—but for endless ifs—
might have missed out on being alive
together with marvels and follies
and longings and lies and wishes
and error and humor and mercy
and journeys and voices and faces
and colors and summers and mornings
and knowledge and tears and chance.

BEGINNING WITH 1914

Since it always begins
in the unlikeliest place,
we start in an obsolete country
on no current map. The camera
glides over flower beds,
for this is a southern climate.
We focus on medals, a horse,
on a white uniform,
for this is June. The young man
waves to the people lining the road,
he lifts a child, he catches
a rose from a wrinkled woman
in a blue kerchief. Then we hear shots
and close in on a casket
draped in the Austrian flag.
Thirty-one days torn off a calendar.
Bombs on Belgrade; then Europe explodes.
We watch the trenches fill with men,
the air with live ammunition.
A close-up of a five-year-old
living on turnips. Her older sister,
my not-yet-mother, already
wearing my daughter's eyes,
is reading a letter as we cut
to a young man with thick glasses
who lies in a trench and writes
a study of Ibsen. I recognize him,
he is going to be my father,
and this is his way of keeping alive.

Snow. Blood. Lice. Frostbite.
Grenades. Stretchers. Coffins. Snow.
Telegrams with black borders.
On the wide screen my father returns
bringing his brother's body;
my mother's father brings back his son's
from the opposite edge. They come together
under the oaks of the cemetery.

All who will be my family
are here, except my sister,
who is not yet imagined.
Neither am I, who imagine
this picture, who now jump
to my snowy birthday in the year
of the million-mark loaf of bread.
My early years are played
by a blue-eyed child who grows up
quickly, for this is a film
of highlights, like all documentaries
false to the life—the work
of selective memory, all I can bear
of a painful childhood. The swastika
appears and remains as the huge
backdrop against which we're seen.
The sound track of a hysterical voice
is threatening us. We're heard as whispers.
Shortly before my city
bursts into flames, my stand-in
disappears from the film, which continues
with scenes of terror and death

I can't bear to watch. I pick up
a new reel, a strange sequel
set in a different location
and made in another language,
in which I am back. The colors are bright,
the sound track is filled with music,
the focus gentle. A man is beside me.
Time-lapse photography picks up
the inchmeal growth of daughters
toward the sky, the slow subversion
of dark by gray hair. Little happens.
The camera sums up the even flow
of many years in a shot of a river.
The principals from part one
are missing, except for me
who am the connection. The time is now,
and I am playing myself.

MERCE CUNNINGHAM
AND THE BIRDS

Last night I saw Merce Cunningham and his ten amazing dancers
dancing for eighty minutes without a break in the college gym.

I am trying to tell you how it was
    but of course there are no words
    for being wholly enclosed in a space,
    a tight cocoon without chinks
    so none of the wonder will leak out

Instead, I ask you to watch the assorted birds
feeding outside this window,
darting and dropping and zeroing in,
assuming positions in groups of threes
    or fours, to break up and form
    new patterns, other groups

how each incessant performer
signals a personal flash of color:
cardinal red, jay blue,
towhee orange, March pea green
    of not-yet-yellow goldfinch,
always tempered with black

how even their silences prefigure
shifts already known to the muscles

    and how none leads or follows
    how each moves

to the authority of its brain

its autonomous body

perpetual proof that the world

is energy, that to land

in a certain space at a certain time

is being alive; watch how they manage

to keep it up till each soul is fed

and disappear into nowhere

WHY WE TELL STORIES
For Linda Nemec Foster

1

Because we used to have leaves
and on damp days
our muscles feel a tug,
painful now, from when roots
pulled us into the ground

and because our children believe
they can fly, an instinct retained
from when the bones in our arms
were shaped like zithers and broke
neatly under their feathers

and because before we had lungs
we knew how far it was to the bottom
as we floated open-eyed
like painted scarves through the scenery
of dreams, and because we awakened

and learned to speak

2

We sat by the fire in our caves,
and because we were poor, we made up a tale
about a treasure mountain
that would open only for us

and because we were always defeated,
we invented impossible riddles
only we could solve,
monsters only we could kill,
women who could love no one else

and because we had survived
sisters and brothers, daughters and sons,
we discovered bones that rose
from the dark earth and sang
as white birds in the trees

3

Because the story of our life
becomes our life

Because each of us tells
the same story
but tells it differently

and none of us tells it
the same way twice

Because grandmothers looking like spiders
want to enchant the children
and grandfathers need to convince us
what happened happened because of them

and though we listen only
haphazardly, with one ear,
we will begin our story
with the word *and*

VOYAGER
For my father, 1897–1976

No one's body could be that light,
not even after it burns—
I know this is not you,
has nothing to do with you

I know you stand on a ship
looking through the eyeholes
nearsighted and patient as always,
still knowing everything

No matter what language they speak,
the boatmen in the black barges
that pass you, you will answer

No matter what bundle of time
they inhabit, you will direct them,
warn them once more and once more in vain

You who changed countries more often than shoes
can step ashore anywhere;
loneliness is the anchor
you've always carried with you

*

The desert is what I would have spared you,
the wilderness after my mother died,
your fixed star

Everything could be borne,
all knowledge, all separation
except that final one

Slowly you turned to stone

And I, your daughter/keeper—
what did I know about
the sentience of stone?

I watered you with indignities
and tears, but you never bloomed

Now both of you have entered
the history of your photographs;
together, young and smiling,
you stand on the steps of Notre Dame
"These are my parents, friends, and children,"
I say, but it is hopeless

I want the impossible photograph,
one that would show the world
your trick, how you and she
pulled joy from any borrowed hat
or sleeve, a survivor's art

This is the hardest knowledge:
that no one will remember you
when your daughters are gone

*

Five years before you died
I took your picture;
you were wearing a dark jacket
and your hair was white

Now I hold the negative
up to the light and the sun streams through
as though it were Notre Dame again,
the rose window

You are changed, you wear
the pale clothes of summer,
your skin and hair are black

How can you see, your glasses
are whitewashed and there are holes
where your teeth used to be

Nevertheless you smile at me
across an enormous distance
as you have so many times
to let me know you have arrived

SOUTHPAW

"Were you an only child?" she asks.
No, but you've always favored the dreamer,
the star pitcher who writes novels,
the prophet with the red armband,
the low notes of the piano,
the swimmer against the stream.

You learned the truth early, that handles
are on the other side,
that doors are hinged to slow your entrance
and gloves and gadgets are made for others,
but you know that the ancient tools—
jugs, spoons, hammers, rakes—
care only about your opposable thumb.

It's your birthright, the extra effort
you've secretly come to love.
"Left, left," the drill sergeant stutters,
and you smile like one of the chosen.
You push the reluctant ballpoint
forward, while the letters wave back,
and taste the word *sinister* on your tongue.
How enchanting it is, so sensuous,
the song of a mermaid with two left arms.

AFTER WHISTLER

There are girls who should have been swans.
At birth their feathers are burned;
their human skins never fit.
When the other children
line up on the side of the sun,
they will choose the moon,
that precious aberration.
They are the daughters mothers
worry about. All summer,
dressed in gauze, they flicker
inside the shaded house,
drawn to the mirror, where their eyes,
two languid moths, hang dreaming.
It's winter they wait for, the first snowfall
with the steady interior hum
only they can hear;
they stretch their arms, as if they were wounded,
toward the bandages of snow.
Briefly, the world is theirs
in its perfect frailty

SCENIC ROUTE
For Lucy, who called them "ghost houses"

Someone was always leaving
and never coming back.
The wooden houses wait like old wives
along this road; they are everywhere,
abandoned, leaning, turning gray.

Someone always traded
the lonely beauty
of hemlock and stony lakeshore
for survival, packed up his life
and drove off to the city.
In the yards the apple trees
keep hanging on, but the fruit
grows smaller year by year.

When we come this way again
the trees will have gone wild,
the houses collapsed, not even worth
the human act of breaking in.
Fields will have taken over.

What we will recognize
is the wind, the same fierce wind,
which has no history.

MONET REFUSES
THE OPERATION

Doctor, you say there are no halos
around the streetlights in Paris
and what I see is an aberration
caused by old age, an affliction.
I tell you it has taken me all my life
to arrive at the vision of gas lamps as angels,
to soften and blur and finally banish
the edges you regret I don't see,
to learn that the line I called the horizon
does not exist and sky and water,
so long apart, are the same state of being.
Fifty-four years before I could see
Rouen cathedral is built
of parallel shafts of sun,
and now you want to restore
my youthful errors: fixed
notions of top and bottom,
the illusion of three-dimensional space,
wisteria separate
from the bridge it covers.
What can I say to convince you
the Houses of Parliament dissolve
night after night to become
the fluid dream of the Thames?
I will not return to a universe
of objects that don't know each other,
as if islands were not the lost children
of one great continent. The world

is flux, and light becomes what it touches,

becomes water, lilies on water,

above and below water,

becomes lilac and mauve and yellow

and white and cerulean lamps,

small fists passing sunlight

so quickly to one another

that it would take long, streaming hair

inside my brush to catch it.

To paint the speed of light!

Our weighted shapes, these verticals,

burn to mix with air

and change our bones, skin, clothes

to gases. Doctor,

if only you could see

how heaven pulls earth into its arms

and how infinitely the heart expands

to claim this world, blue vapor without end.

THERE ARE MORNINGS

Even now, when the plot
calls for me to turn to stone,
the sun intervenes. Some mornings
in summer I step outside
and the sky opens
and pours itself into me
as if I were a saint
about to die. But the plot
calls for me to live,
be ordinary, say nothing
to anyone. Inside the house
the mirrors burn when I pass.

MISSING THE DEAD

I miss the old scrawl on the viaduct,
the crazily dancing red letters: BIRD LIVES.
It's gone now, the wall as clean as forgetting.
I go home and put on a record,
Charlie Parker Live at the Blue Note.
Each time I play it, months or years apart,
the music emerges more luminous;
I never listened so well before.

I wish my parents had been musicians
and left me themselves transformed into sound,
or that I could believe in the stars
as the radiant bodies of the dead.
Then I could stand in the dark, pointing out
my mother and father to all
who did not know them, how they shimmer,
how they keep getting brighter
as we keep moving toward each other.

WHEN I AM ASKED

When I am asked
how I began writing poems,
I talk about the indifference of nature.

It was soon after my mother died,
a brilliant June day,
everything blooming.

I sat on a gray stone bench
in a lovingly planted garden,
but the day lilies were as deaf
as the ears of drunken sleepers
and the roses curved inward.
Nothing was black or broken
and not a leaf fell
and the sun blared endless commercials
for summer holidays.

I sat on a gray stone bench
ringed with the ingenue faces
of pink and white impatiens
and placed my grief
in the mouth of language,
the only thing that would grieve with me.

LETTER FROM THE END
OF THE WORLD

The reason no longer matters,
the lamp, my curiosity,
my sisters' insinuations,
never waking up together,
you saying, "Trust me."

The point is the end of innocence
comes when you look at someone you love
asleep and see how his eyeballs flicker
under their shallow lids.

The point is since I lost you
I have been going around the world
looking for you and finding myself
instead, small scraps of a woman
that are beginning to fit.

At first the mountains closed ranks against me,
blackberries dried in my mouth,
the wind kept turning to face me.
Wherever I came, the music stopped,
sidewalks opened up manholes,
lights went out,
a pregnant woman shielded her face.

But I learned to sleep on the ground
despite the heartbeat of giant oaks
and the moon's soft taunts at the sun,

the all-night labor of heaving roots,
the mushroom smell of death.

I learned not to throw the bouquets
the wretched made of their wounds
back in their faces, to accept
tears brought me on red pillows,
to knock on plain white doors
without windows or peepholes, not knowing
whose voice would say, "Come in."

The point is I came back
from the deep places. Always
there was help, a man or woman
who asked no questions, an animal's
warm body, the itch in my muscles
to climb a swinging rope.

I started out as a girl
without a shadow, in iron shoes;
now, at the end of the world
I am a woman full of rain.
The journey back should be easy;
if this reaches you, wait for me.

CAVALLERIA RUSTICANA

All the fireflies in the world
are gathered in our yard tonight,
flickering in the shrubs
like an ostentatious display
of Christmas lights out of season.
But the music in the air
is the music of heat, of August—
cicadas scraping out
their thin, harsh treble
like country fiddlers settling in
for a long night. I feel at home
with their relentless tune,
minimalist, like the eighties.

Events repeat themselves,
but with a difference that makes all
the difference. As a child,
one summer night in Verona
at my first opera,
I watched a swarm of matches
light up the Roman arena
until we were silent. It was as if
music were a night-blooming flower
that would not open
until we held our breath.
Then the full-blown sound,
the single-minded combat
of passion: voices sharpening
their glittering blades on one another,

electing to live or die.

It was that simple. The story was

of no importance, the motive lost

in the sufficient, breathing dark.

If there was a moon I don't remember.

INTO SPACE

How light we are becoming

Our diets of greens and seeds
hollow us, bring us closer
to the birds;
our buoyant winter coats
are stuffed for luck
with incipient feathers.

Everything in our lives
is thinning down, prepares itself
for the weightless future.

Lasers replace cumbersome tools,
boxes diminish to buttons;
soon our messy, erroneous hearts
will be superseded
and the gigantic god
of history dwarfed to a nylon tape
we carry in our pockets.

*

Like mountain climbers and athletes,
we undergo daily training

We go out in the morning
and when we return
our houses are thirty stories high,

our names not listed
in the lobby

We float to the top of the building,
naked in glass elevators,
and when we emerge our neighbors
meet us with guns, just in case

They look at us round-eyed
and ask who we are

Back on the street, our feet
lift off the ground, the trees
and lampposts we reach for back off
into the painted distance

*

In a recurrent dream
I am asked to step out of my shoes,
fold and stack my clothes,
place the contents of my purse
on a desk for later disposal.
I leave my daughter's photographed hands,
my other daughter's new poem,
my keys, my driver's license
with the bad picture, my Chinese
address book with its birds and flowers.
Strip-searched, I am forced to surrender
my mother's bookmark of dried heather
taped to the sole of my foot
and my husband's twenty-year-old face

in a heart-shaped locket concealed in my hair.
Finally, when I step on the scales
no lights flash;
the X-ray scanner sweeps over me
and finds me empty.

*

Think of the sac of memory
as the last resort,
the bundle the refugees tie to a stick
when they cross the frozen river

Think of the contents, volatile
as dandelion fluff
when we finally scatter it
into the atmosphere we are leaving

Think of it falling on someone
who suspects nothing,
who is suddenly moved to recall
a forgotten childhood scene
and finds himself stunned by its gravity.

NOCTURNE

Sometimes, in the dead of night, I wake up in an immense hole of silence. Then I wait, with hope and dread, for the first sound to drop into it. Hope for something benign: the soothing background music of rain, or an owl's throaty signal. Dread of a wailing siren, or the telephone, which at this hour could bring me only a thick, demented voice, or the impersonal speech issuing from some desk of disaster. Last night, when it came, it was a sound of blessing, the rough-and-tumble bumping-together of freight cars in the switchyard down the road—that simple, artless coupling, and a long time later, the drawn-out, low-voiced hum of the train rolling down the single track. Sounds of work, of confidence in the night, in getting from here to there. Sounds of connection; sweet music. I lay there and listened to the moonless night fill up with sound until the darkness throbbed with a dream of arrival.

Jacob Love

Poetry

Dependencies. U of North Carolina P, 1965.

Life of a Queen. Juniper Press, 1970.

(with Dave Etter). *Voyages to the Inland Sea: Essays and Poems.* Edited by John Judson, Center for Contemporary Poetry, 1971.

The Private Life. Louisiana State UP, 1975.

Voices from the Forest. Juniper Press, 1977.

The Need to Hold Still. Louisiana State UP, 1980.

Second Language. Louisiana State UP, 1986.

Waving from Shore. Louisiana State UP, 1989.

Learning to Play by Ear: Essays and Early Poems. Juniper Press, 1990.

Alive Together: New and Selected Poems. Louisiana State UP, 1996.

Translations

Kaschnitz, Marie Luise. *Selected Later Poems of Marie Luise Kaschnitz.* Princeton UP, 1980.

———. *Whether or Not.* Juniper Press, 1984.

———. *Circe's Mountain: Stories by Marie Luise Kaschnitz.* Milkweed Press, 1990.

Mitgutsch, Anna. *Three Daughters.* Harcourt Brace, 1987.

Society for the Study of MIDWESTERN LITERATURE

2025 Symposium of Scholars and Creative Writers

CALL FOR PROPOSALS

- literary criticism
- creative writing

DEADLINE
~~February 1, 2025~~
February 28, 2025

with a Midwestern emphasis

MAY 29–30

2025

- papers/posters
- panels
- round tables

QUESTIONS?
Jeff Hotz
jhotz@esu.edu

See ssml.org for submission instructions.

WRITING THE MIDWEST

Kellogg Hotel and Convention Center

East Lansing, MI

CALL FOR PROPOSALS

The GREAT GATSBY

1925 was a banner year for Midwestern literature. Important novels published that year include F. Scott Fitzgerald's *The Great Gatsby*, Willa Cather's *The Professor's House*, Ernest Hemingway's *In Our Time*, Theodore Dreiser's *An American Tragedy*, and Sinclair Lewis's *Arrowsmith*. To celebrate the 100th anniversary of this important year, the Society for the Study of Midwestern Literature invites essay proposals for a special issue of its peer-reviewed journal *Midwestern Miscellany* on the topic of "Midwestern Literature in 1925," to be edited by Scott Emmert (University of Wisconsin Oshkosh). Proposals may focus on the famous novels of 1925 or texts / authors that have been overshadowed by Fitzgerald, Cather, Hemingway, Dreiser, and Lewis.

F·SCOTT·FITZGERALD

Proposals should be no more than 300 words and should include a brief critical bibliography. Completed essays should be between 3,000 and 5,000 words. Contributors must be members of SSML before publication.

PROPOSAL DEADLINE	ESSAY DEADLINE
January 1, 2025	August 1, 2025

Send proposal and short CV to Scott Emmert (emmerts@uwosh.edu). Please also indicate if you would like your proposal to be considered for a special panel at the 2025 Symposium of the Society for the Study of Midwestern Literature (May 29-30, East Lansing, MI).

NEED SOME INSPIRATION? LESSER KNOWN TEXTS PUBLISHED IN 1925

Bess Streeter Aldrich, *The Rim of the Prairie*
Sherwood Anderson, *Dark Laughter*
Lorna Doone Beers, *Prairie Fires*
Earl Derr Biggers, *The House Without a Key*
Thomas A. Boyd, *Samuel Drummond*
Louis Bromfield, *Possession*
Hallie Quinn Brown, *Tales My Father Told*
Edgar Rice Burroughs, *The Moon Men*
Edgar Rice Burroughs, *The Red Hawk*
Floyd Dell, *This Mad Ideal* and *Runaway*
John Dos Passos, *Manhattan Transfer*
Geoffrey Dell Eaton, *Backfurrow*
T. S. Eliot, "The Hollow Men"
John T. Frederick, *Green Bush*
Ruth Gaines-Shelton, "The Church Fight"
Zane Grey, *The Vanishing American*
John Herrmann, *Foreign Born*

Emerson Hough, *The Ship of Souls*
Langston Hughes, "The Weary Blues"
Alain Locke (ed.), *The New Negro*
Archibald Macleish, *The Pot of Earth*
Walter J. Mullenburg, *Prairie*
Martha Ostenso, *Wild Geese*
O.E. Rolvaag, *Giants in the Earth*
Helen Hooven Santmeyer, *Herbs and Apples*
James Stevens, *Paul Bunyan*
Gene Stratton-Porter, *The Keeper of the Bees*
Ruth Suckow, *The Odyssey of a Nice Girl*
Ruth Plumly Thompson, *The Lost King of Oz*
Jim Tully, *Jarnegan*
Carl Van Vechten, *Firecrackers: A Realistic Novel*
Glenway Wescott, *Natives of Rock*
Harold Bell Wright, *A Son of the Father*
Little magazines: *Poetry, The Midland*, etc.

CFP: Reading and Writing the Midwest

Recent essays in popular publications such as *The Atlantic*, *The New York Times*, and *Psychology Today* have sounded the alarm that college students today cannot read. Is this true? The Society for the Study of Midwestern Literature calls for proposals for an upcoming issue of *Midwestern Miscellany* devoted to the topic of "Reading and Writing the Midwest," to be edited by Catherine Clifford (Hastings College) and Rachael Price (Abraham Baldwin Agricultural College).

Successful essays will describe a specific challenge in the classroom and/or a successful classroom activity or assignment; evaluate a theory of reading, writing, literacy, or pedagogy; or examine a text or historical moment related to literacy in the Midwest. Please send proposals (max. 300 words) and short CV to Catherine Clifford (cat.clifford@hastings.edu) and Rachael Price (rprice @abac.edu) by April 1, 2025. Finished essays (3,000-7,000 words) will be due by July 1, 2025.

Topics may include, but are not limited to, the following:

- Midwestern texts that engage students or promote specific reading skills
- Writing about the Midwest or place
- Responses to think pieces about university students and reading and/or writing
- Debates about early reading instruction (such as the Science of Reading and/or Whole Language reading)
- Theories of literacy, as they apply to midwestern classrooms and/or texts
- Theories of composition, including multimodal composition and accessibility, as they apply to midwestern classrooms and/or texts
- Use of generative AI in higher ed classrooms
- Theories of evaluation, such as anti-racist or equity-minded grading, in higher ed
- Debates about school choice, charter schools, or parents' rights bills in the Midwest

SSML Annual Symposium

Please send a proposal and short CV to Rachael Price (rprice@abac.edu) and Patricia Oman (poman@hastings.edu) by Feb 25, 2025, if you would like to be considered for a panel on the same topic at this year's symposium of the Society for the Study of Midwestern Literature (May 29-30, 2025, at the Kellog Hotel and Conference Center, East Lansing, Michigan).

*AI-generated image of Midwestern higher ed classroom with laptops.

www.ingramcontent.com/pod-product-compliance
Lightning Source LLC
Chambersburg PA
CBHW061705120626
46550CB00003B/1094